Saving Our Sons from The Traps of the Enemy

SARAH HALEY

authorHOUSE·

AuthorHouse™
1663 Liberty Drive
Bloomington, IN 47403
www.authorhouse.com
Phone: 833-262-8899

Published by AuthorHouse 10/23/2020

ISBN: 978-1-6655-0513-0 (sc)
ISBN: 978-1-6655-0512-3 (e)

Print information available on the last page.

Any people depicted in stock imagery provided by Getty Images are models, and such images are being used for illustrative purposes only. Certain stock imagery © Getty Images.

This book is printed on acid-free paper.

CONTENTS

Foreword.. vii

Preface ix

Introduction.. xi

Chapter 1   Nail-Tech Palm Reader 1

Chapter 2   I Could Hear God Speaking to Me for Years 5

Chapter 3   Abraham's Story..19

Chapter 4   My Mother 25

Chapter 5   Mrs. Naomi Grace- The Lamb 35

Chapter 6   At Grandma's House During the Summer..................... 42

Chapter 7   Children 44

Chapter 8   Encouraging the Ex, Susan 55

Chapter 9   Clients Talking in the Salon 66

Chapter 10   The Word of God Works................................. 71

Chapter 11   Department of Human Services.......................... 82

Chapter 12   My Husband and I Started a Nonprofit Organization 84

Chapter 13   Questions to Ask Yourself............................... 87

Chapter 14   It's Finished.. 92

About the Author.. 97

FOREWORD

God always has a way of putting you in the right place at the right time. Such is the case with me and my dear friend of over thirty-five years, Sarah Haley. Sarah and I have been together through the ups and the downs of our lives. Many people in life are searching for fame and fortune, not so with Sarah. For the thirty-five years I have known her, of all her desires her strongest desire has been to be a mother. For years she sought God, fasted, prayed, and sought medical opinions. But it was not in God's plan for her to be a mother, at least not in the sense you would expect. Then she met the love of her life, Abraham Haley, who had three sons from a previous marriage.

With so much going on in the world, especially the challenges faced by Young African American Males, *Saving Our Sons from the Traps of the Enemy* is a perfect book for parents raising males and parents raising a blended family. *Saving Our Sons from the Traps of the Enemy* follows the hurts, pains, mistakes, frustrations, anger, disappointments, love, and understanding of a praying and believing Step Mother who only wanted the best for her sons. It also shows her determination to keep her sons from falling into the traps and plans of the enemy, Satan. There is no one better to share their story and offer some of the inciteful wisdom she gained on her journey as a mother. She gave her all for her boys.

This book will bless those who read it. It will encourage those who need it. And most of all, it will assure you that you can Save Your Sons from the Traps of the Enemy.

Dr. Leo Johnson
Dr. Renae Johnson
Memphis, Tennessee

PREFACE

A Fire Started in Me

Early one sunshiny Sunday morning, April 21, 2019, my apostle, Dr. D. Jackson, senior leader at our church, was preaching on 2 Corinthians 4:7 (KJV): "But we have this treasure in earthen vessels, that the excellency of the power may be of God, and not of us."

In Dr. Jackson's introduction, he spoke on finding passion and purpose in life. At that moment, I thought, *What am I willing to die for?* In my heart, that's what I used to say about our boys when they were six and four years old. I have done that, and I died to myself to obey God. I was willing to die rather than watch our boys be destroyed by our enemy and adversary, Satan.

I sat there in church thinking how my apostle would answer that question: passion and purpose in life. I can't think of anything else I'm willing to die for and have a passion for. I did have a passion for doing hair. In 1987, I went to beauty school, and after receiving my cosmetology license from the Alabama State Board of Cosmetology, I had opened a salon. I'd been a hair stylist for thirty-two years. But what was next?

So I started fasting and praying. It seemed as though every place I went, people wanted an update on our sons. They would reminisce about things that had happened at the salon. Clients would say, "Susan did this or that," Susan being the biological mother. Or they would say things like, "I'm so happy that you and your husband took those children out of their situation. Girl, I applaud you guys. I couldn't have done it. You are a better woman than I." At that moment, I would say I was just doing what God told me to do. Every day, two or three times a day, I had to tell my story, and I was tired of it.

One morning, I was driving to work praying about my passion, my purpose; I said to God, "I've done it." God said, "Write about it. It's your life. It's your story and nobody else's, and your story will help others who are having to do the same thing that I commanded you to do."

I have never written a book before, but I do know my story. God will help me. I told myself that I never had opened a salon before, and God helped me do that. I know He is the same God yesterday, today, and forever more. God did it before, and He can do it again, as written in Hebrews 13:8.

The passion and purpose is in me to share and help be a blessing to others. I must tell them how the Gospel of Jesus Christ strengthened me during all those years of hurt, pain, disappointment, and sacrifice that I went through. Our sons were also worth the fight, worth saving, and so are your children.

Many people miss the will of God for their lives because they are afraid or selfish and want to play it safe. At the end of life, they find themselves saying things like, "I was safe, but I'm sorry" or "I wish I could turn back the hands of time—I would have helped those children." What risk will you take in order to obey God? Know the plan God has for you.

INTRODUCTION

The Holy Spirit revealed to me that what I did years ago for Him was my mission and purpose—being a mom to children I didn't birth and protecting them from the traps of the enemy. There are so many more children waiting to be set free from Satan's traps. Many parents are not willing to rise up and get involved in their children's lives; they don't realize they can avoid a lot of long-term pain and heartache.

This book is for single parents, married couples, and blended families of all ages. Males, females, African Americans, Caucasians, Hispanics, and all other ethnicities can read it if they need a push or more encouragement to rise up and take on the challenge. I'm targeting members of any socio-economic status.

My book will encourage readers' prayer lives. I believe readers will be influenced to have tenacity to take a stand and be a success in their children's lives. In the future, readers can use my book as a reference guide to go back to. They will be grateful for following their own hearts to save the children. The scriptures for spiritual guidance will support the ideas in my book. Readers will be encouraged to do spiritual warfare without fear when the time comes.

Yes, we can save our blended families. Readers will discover that, if the Spirit is being moved in them for this kind of assignment, God has already prepared them through their upbringing for the challenge. God has allowed some loving relatives to deposit some wonderful life-changing seeds already deep inside of them. If they think and dig, they will see.

CHAPTER 1

———•———

Nail-Tech Palm Reader

In 1989, I was working at a salon called Total Image in Atlanta, Georgia. One day I asked the nail tech to give me a manicure. She said, "Sit down, and I'll do it." I sat in the chair, and she began to stare at my hands as she held them, looking at my fingers and nails and wrists.

She said, "Oh my. Oh, oh, oh, no … So you like that guy who's been coming by and parks his eighteen-wheeler on the side of the building?"

I said, "Yes, I do."

She said, "Don't marry him."

I said, "Why? What's wrong with him? He's a sweet guy. I know he is the guy for me. I have seen him in a dream."

She said, "I can read your future."

I was so surprised. I hadn't known she was a palm reader. If I had, I probably would not have sat in her chair. "What?"

She said, "Please don't marry him. His ex-wife is going to torture you so bad—oh, it's going to be bad. Please! I'm warning you—don't marry this guy."

I was young, only twenty-four years old. I didn't know a lot of scripture at all, but I was saved, and I did know that my God has all power. So I said to her, "Tell me, what will God be doing while the devil is using her to torture me?" She couldn't say. I said, "Can you see that?" She had no answer. I said, "God will help me. God will be with me. I believe in God, so I will trust Him in this."

Do not listen to a palm reader. They see the work of the enemy. They have only limited information. There are going to be trials and troubles in this life on earth. Whether you get married, whether you stay single, you can't avoid them. They just show up to make us stronger and more powerful witnesses. Psalm 34:19 says, "Many are the afflictions of the righteous, but the Lord shall deliver us from them all" (KJV). We become disciples and make more disciples.

In 1989, I asked God, "Who is my husband?" I wrote to God on paper:

> God I want a man that don't smoke, don't drink, love you God, no whore, and no couch potato and work hard. He does not have to be in church but willing to go with me and love me as Christ loves the church. If my future husband has kids, I'll love them and help them the best way I can.

I told God that my dream was to open a hair salon and to work hard, make lots of money, and purchase a town house just for two. My dream car was a Corvette. I wanted to travel the world and live like King Solomon—an extravagant life. Then I added: "I don't want an ugly man, so ugly I can't look at him."

I said that because a lady who was very close to me said she had prayed and asked God for an ugly man so the other women wouldn't look at him. I said to myself right then (I was a teenager), *I will never pray that prayer.* The lady's prayer was answered. I wrote out my desires two times. I put one note on my refrigerator and one on the dashboard of my car. When I shifted gears in my five-speed Nissan Sentra, I would read it out loud and say, "God, you said in the Book of Habakkuk, chapter two, second verse, "Write the vision and make it plain on tablets so he may run who reads it" (KJV).

So I did just that. I would read it every time I opened my refrigerator and every time I drove my car. I would cry out loud because I was lonely and wanted to have a great guy in my life, somebody I could love and share my life with. I was working in a salon. I was twenty-four years old and making five or six hundred dollars a week. I had my own apartment, my own car; I served the Lord and sang in the choir. I was watching young men teach the Bible and saying to myself, *That's the kind of man I want to have in my life—nice suits and ties, nice shoes, talking about my God, Jesus Christ, whom I love.*

One day I was combing my hair in the mirror and found myself thinking, *What good is it to try to make myself look attractive to another no-good guy in my life?* I guess I thought that if I looked ugly—no pretty hairstyle, no makeup—no guys would even want to look at me. I had been feeling sad at the time and losing my self-esteem. But I kept on styling my hair, and suddenly I had a flash of a vision of a man going up the steps of an eighteen-wheeler with five or six kids beside the rig. The man was smiling at me. I said, "Lord, who is this guy and all these little children?"

Not long after that, my sister told me about a guy she wanted me to meet. Six months later, Abraham and I were married. We have been together praising God through trials and tests, highs and lows, for twenty-nine years now, and God is still faithful to us. But less than three months after we married, I was about to have an annulment. I was afraid that my mother would come out of me, or my mean granddaddy, Lawson Fenoil. I thank God I stayed; I thank God I listened to the Spirit. The Holy Spirit spoke to me so clearly, saying, "No, don't do that—stay with him and make sure Susan doesn't destroy him and the kids. I have a plan for you. Stay, and I will bless you."

When I heard the voice I was blown away. "What?" I asked. He spoke again to me, twice the same thing.

Susan was my husband's ex-wife. She would talk to Abraham in such an ugly way. She was used to him jumping every time she screamed, "I want! I need! Do this, Abraham. Do that, Abraham." One day she said, "Didn't we agree that our kids would be first?" What she meant that *she* should be first. "Nobody else will come before our kids—didn't we say that, Abraham?" He just looked and didn't say a word.

I said to myself, *This man is humble; this man is too sweet. I will not allow this loud, immature, selfish lady to disrespect my husband and use manipulation in every situation or use reverse psychology to get her way at the end of the day.* I had heard God say, "Stay." And I said, "Lord, you know I am not that spiritual, but I'm doing it the way I believe You want me to, with a few choice words. Forgive me for cursing—it's in me right now." To Susan I said, "Not anymore, Susan. It's over. Sarah is here now. Don't curse my man out—curse me. I'm ready, born for this. This is my man now; you get a job, sister—quick, fast, and in a hurry. Your child support will be paid."

First of all, Susan was taking all she could take and was mistreating my man. She was getting money from his family too. It was out of control. She told them Abraham would give it back to them.

Second of all, many of his family members and customers were taking advantage of my husband. Cousins were getting cars repaired and not paying. It seemed people were pushing Abraham over, and he was allowing it. God already knew that I wasn't having it. Years later, Abraham started having everyone that he did business with sign a contract before he would do any work for them.

I was the mouthpiece God used in our early years of marriage until my husband grew out of allowing those things to happen. Abraham grew in the Spirit; soon he did change to become a great man of God and became the man God called him to be. Abraham did rise up and start handling his business. Thank God for the Men's Ministry at New Direction.

CHAPTER 2

---·◆·---

I Could Hear God Speaking to Me for Years

God said, "Sarah, I know the plans I have for you, plans to prosper you and give you a hope and a future" (Jeremiah 29:11 KJV).

Mystery of the Dimes

For many years in Nashville, Tennessee, and also in Memphis, Tennessee, everywhere I went, I would find dimes on the ground and on the floors of buildings. When I went shopping, exercising, when I opened the door of my car—dimes, dimes, dimes! One day I mentioned to my husband that I kept finding all these dimes everywhere I went, and he said, "Search it out." What he meant was Proverbs 25:2 KJV (one of his favorite scriptures): "It is the glory of God to conceal a thing, but the honour of kings is to search out a matter." So I searched it out and found that dimes represent many things, and one of them is coming full circle. And dimes also represent guidance or validation that you are on the right path.

Every time I would bend down and pick up a dime, I would hear God say, "I'm giving you double for your trouble." God is praised for being mysterious.

If God showed us some great, unbelievable plan He had for us when we were immature and unable to understand, we would just loose it. When He began to unfold the mysteries (twenty years had gone by), I just couldn't stop praying and crying. He really had to equip me, mature me, and humble me. Another scripture comes to mind: "After you have suffered for a little while the God of all grace will himself, will make you perfect, establish you, strengthen and settle you" (1 Peter 5:10 KJV). After some years, I said, "Lord, haven't I suffered a little while?" God said, "A little while more." His little while and our little while are not the same, not at all. Another scripture comes to mind: <u>"His ways are not our ways, His thoughts are not our thoughts, says the Lord. As the heavens are higher than the earth, so are my ways higher than yours"</u> (Isaiah 55:8–9 KJV). If you think you're going to get some quick, deep answers from God, you'll discover that some answers do not come so quickly. I couldn't get quick answers, and you can't either. We must become God chasers and God seekers. We must pray without ceasing, living for God and loving God for who He is and not just to get a quick fix. He will give us things and supply needs. He says, <u>"I have given you everything you need pertaining to life and godliness according to"</u> (2 Peter 1:3 KJV). We must love people! How can we do something great for God if we hate people? I'm talking about deep things that pertain to His overall plan for you concerning who you really are, and where He is taking you. He has anointed you for His glory and in His divine timing. Chase God. Ask questions if you want to know. We must know what God has appointed us to. God anoints, and He appoints.

Too Many Memories to Forget

It's a beautiful picture now. Better is the end of a thing than the beginning thereof (Ecclesiastes 7:8)

All I seem to do some days is think about our sons. I think about how well they are doing today. I smile as I look up at men now, mature handsome young men working, taking care of their families. Sometimes

I cry tears of joy. I look up toward heaven and say, "God, you helped Abraham and I to do this." It's over now. It's like a big dream in my mind, but it really did happen. I think of all the places we went—trips out of town, vacations, driving them to school when they were kids. We had so many life-changing conversations on those trips to and from school. Even though I worked long hours when the boys were growing up, they never missed a meal. When they came into the salon after school, they could smell something cooking in the Crock-Pot*. I can remember it as if it was yesterday—frying potatoes in a FryDaddy* and running back there taking them out of the grease. They would ask, "Are they ready? Are they ready?" Every time we get together, we talk about when they were growing up. They hated those cute outfits we bought them. They said the outfits made them look like the Walton boys from a television series called *The Waltons*. A lady at our church started that; they were so mad at that lady. She was complimenting their clothes and said, "Oh look at y'all with those Walton boy outfits ... nice outfits!" When we all get together now, the conversation is always about when they were growing up. And we will find ourselves laughing about so many different situations. The pain is not with me anymore, but I remember almost every situation, good and bad. I can't just keep trying to tell it all. I would rather write a book that will help me remember and also help families that may be facing some of the same things I have overcome. I want to see my friends and readers of this book win and save their sons and daughters from the traps of the enemy.

God made me a super woman. I'm fifty-five now, and I say, "*Wow!* How did it happen?" It's been twenty-nine years now.

In 1996, God said, "Move out of the house at 855 Straight Street, Huntsville. Move into an apartment." I didn't like hearing that! I said, "God, is this You or the devil? If it's You, we will move. If it's the devil we will stay and stand on the Word." I said, "Lord, show me." God gave me a dream: I saw angels in white linen clothing on white horses. They came to the windows of our house and carried us out one by one. I woke up and told Abraham, "God wants us to move out." I cried so hard, but we were obedient. Then I began to hear God say, <u>"And every one that hath forsaken houses, or brethren, or sisters, or father, or mother, or wife, or children, or lands, for my name's sake, shall receive an hundredfold, and shall inherit everlasting life"</u> (Matthew 19:29 KJV).

My Plans Interrupted

"Many plans are in a man's heart" (Proverbs 19:21 NASB). My plans were for a small townhouse instead of a four-bedroom house. My dream car was a Corvette, but with three boys, I ended up with a van. After living in the house on Straight Street for a few years, God said, "Let the house go and seek another man's wealth." In other words, he wanted us to move into an apartment. As if letting the house go wasn't enough, then God said, "When the lease is up on the van, do not renew it." My husband had a preaching engagement in Huntsville one Sunday, and we had to borrow our apostle's Blazer. While we were riding to the church, I heard God say, "The next time you get in this truck, it will be yours." I told my husband what I'd heard God say. He looked at me as if I was crazy and said, "This Blazer is like new." It was a 1996 model, and the year was 1997. I said, "Yes it is, but I heard God. Wait. You'll see." Soon—maybe two to three weeks later—our pastor made an announcement that God said he was to give his Blazer to the Haley family. If I hear God, you can best believe what he says *will* come to pass.

1999—My Life Was Changing

I was living better, loving people better, talking better, worshiping and praising God, and having a relationship with God. I was praying more, trusting God. I saw all this as a beautiful life if I could ever get there.

My salon business was going under. I went to my apostle and asked him to take it over so I wouldn't lose it completely. He said God had already shown him the same thing. I came to him in a dream and asked him for help and to take over my salon.

I was so miserable. I still was cursing, hating and angry all the time. The kids required so much. Susan had hurt me to the core. My bills got behind; clients were leaving calling me crazy, a fool. My head was down. I went from making $1,500 to $2,000 a week to making $27 for a whole week. Like Humpty Dumpty who sat on the wall, I had a great fall.

God told me in a dream to keep my eyes on Him; only then would I not drown. He told me to get in the water. I said, "I can't swim! I will drown!" I was losing it. God said, "You will not drown if you keep your eyes on Me." I was so distracted by so many people asking the same question over and over again: "It's not your salon anymore?" In 2000 the whole city was talking. Pastor D. Jackson had taken Sarah's salon. God spoke to me to give it to our church because I was not making enough money to pay the bills. It was painful, but I did it. "Sarah has lost her mind." I tried hard to explain what the real truth was, but no one believed me. I kept saying, "My apostle didn't take the salon; I gave it up because I wasn't making enough money to pay the bills anymore."

God Was Still Faithful

One day before I gave the salon over to the church, I was sitting in my styling chair, and God spoke so clearly: "Sarah, you get out of the way. I don't need you to provide. I am your Provider. Look to me." My flesh was strong; I thought it was all about me. God used a young lady who had four small kids and who was receiving benefits from the Women, Infants, and Children program (WIC). The young lady said, "Sarah, you have been on my mind for some reason. I have three gallons of milk for you and the kids. My children are too small for this much milk." Then she said, "Since you make so much money, I was afraid to stop by your salon." All I could say was thank you, with tears rolling out my eyes. God was humbling me and teaching me. I had made so much money, I had become prideful. And we all know pride comes before the fall!

God also sent a lady to Winners Medallions, our after-school nonprofit organization. She had a lot of food and boxes of cereal. Right as I was praying one day about how I needed some cereal for the kids, the phone rang. The lady said, "Come over. I have some things for you guys." We all went over—Abraham, the kids and I. She said, "Take whatever you want." I cried again, "Thank you, God." I believe God was saying to me, "I can supply the need without you complaining about how much you have to do and how little their biological momma is doing." Even though I knew God had told me to be a mother to the children, my flesh was weak; I was just upset in my carnal flesh (self). I just still wanted her to do something. It seemed as if a load was on me, and nobody cared. I wasn't a prayer warrior at that time, but because of the church I was attending, I was on my way. It took a while for my mind to be transformed.

At New Direction Church, my apostle taught about transforming my mind and renewing my mind. For years he preached it. It took years for me to get the Word in me. What I should have been saying was, "God provided. God blessed the business. God made a way. God showed up today like He always does."

Plead the Blood of Jesus

We all were in bed asleep. A fire was blazing at the Tasty Gate Shopping Center in the row where my salon was located. The police called me and said they had been trying to reach me. "Your salon is on fire!" I said, "What?" "Your salon is on fire! You need to come right away." I said, "My salon is not on fire, but I will be there in a few minutes." I knew I was right because my heart was not pounding at all. I turned the light on in the boys' room and said, "Put on your house shoes. We have to go to the salon." As I drove to the salon, I told the boys, "The salon cannot be on fire because I have pleaded the blood of Jesus in the salon." I prayed that the Lord would be my covering years ago. I purchased red blinds for the blood. I purchased a red styling chair for the blood, and Abraham painted my walls and put red squares on the floor representing the blood. The fire had started on one end of the shopping center. One shop was burned, and the business next to it had received smoke damage. My salon was next, and there was no damage at all. It did not smell like smoke at all. God honored my prayer and the words I had been speaking over the years. I told the boys, "The blood has power. Did I not say my salon was not on fire?" I praised God, and thanked Him for being faithful to me, and for protecting the salon.

Conqueror

How can you become a conqueror if you never fought in a battle? How can you win if you run from every fight? James 1: 2–3 says, "My brethren,

count it all joy when ye fall into divers temptations; Knowing this, that
the trying of your faith worketh patience" (KJV).

When learning this scripture, I struggled in my flesh. It did not make
sense in my natural understanding, but I kept meditating on it, saying,
"Lord, if you say so." But in the beginning, I was still crying. I said, "Lord,
you say I should count as joy all this pain and mistreatment? Lord, help
me mature. Help me to trust Your word. You know all, and I don't. I will
follow You and keep believing you." God was transforming my mind,
downloading His Word, and removing the old mindset, making me a
new creation.

I always wondered why in the world God would speak to me. At
that time, I was a hot-mess Christian. When I would hear Him, I was so
comforted, but at the same time, I thought I was too carnal for God to use.
He knew I was a babe in Christ who was cursing like a sailor. He knew
there were no scriptures in me. Nevertheless, God was speaking, and as
time progressed, I begin to listen.

I Wanted to Win

I knew I could win. If the Word of God worked for others, then it
could work for me. I just needed to get it in my Spirit and get it activated.
I can recall hearing sermons saying Jesus got up with all power. I had
heard this every Sunday since I was a child. I believed He did get up with
all power, and that means I should have some power too. I just wanted to
live a life so I could operate with some power. I preached a sermon one
Sunday morning at my childhood church. It was called "We Have Power."
Members of the congregation looked at me as if I was crazy. It really hurt
me to know so many people in the church do not believe that God has
given us power. Luke 10:19 says, "I have given you power." I asked the
pastor why. He said, 'Yes, baby, we got power." I said, "No one acts as if
they have power." He said that he felt it was because we don't walk close
enough to God. Something may happen to us if we try to operate in that
kind of power. Read Acts 19:11–20 for a better understanding.

I knew I needed something extra ordinary—Holy Ghost power—to
fight this battle with Susan, the ex-wife. After all the cursing back at her,

I didn't feel victorious. I didn't feel above; rather, I felt beneath. I was sinking, going down more and more to the bottom, not winning at all, not rising, not triumphant, not a conqueror. Apostle Jackson taught us winning strategies. I had to learn the scriptures to win. I wrote them on index cards, and while I was doing hair, I would read them over and over. A friend said, "I see you have scriptures everywhere. Now meditate on what you are reading. Then, when you get it in your belly, out of your belly will flow rivers of living waters." After some time I got it. I was winning.

Stand on the Word

> Isaiah 55:1 KJV: "Come all that is hungry, thirsty, buy, eat that have no money."

"Shop with no money!" He preached this for weeks. This Word was in my mind. I was meditating on it.

We didn't have money for an attorney when we got custody of the last son. We stood on the Word and walked the juvenile court floor praying. We talked with the judge's secretary, told her we didn't have any money for a lawyer. I asked her to ask the judge if he would please see me. It was an emergency. She said, "He doesn't see anyone without a lawyer." But she told him what I'd said. He told her to get my phone number and my address. They mailed a letter to Abraham and me with a date to come to court. "Won't He do it?" Yes, we won the case. We got the fourth son out of that situation. The mother, Susan, was in jail for drug selling when we got him. God turned the king's heart, gave us favor.

What God Told Me and What I Said to God

I said "I'm gonna be so old when I finish this." God said, "Stay in my Word, and my Word will keep your youth."

God said, "Be a mother to those kids." I said, "They have a mother." God said, "I used her as a vehicle to get them here, but I am using you to be a mother—not number one mother, not number two mother—*a* mother." God said, "Stop calling them your stepchildren. Call them your children. I'm giving them to you." I said, "God, I'm not praying to You anymore, because You keep telling me to be a mother to all these children. I am afraid. I never had a baby." (This was my excuse.)

It seemed as if none of this made any sense to me. Every time I got on my knees and started praying, I would hear God say the same thing.

When God called me to preach it was the same sort of thing. I would get on my knees or ride in my car praying. I would hear, "Preach my Word to my people." I just cried. "Lord, I can't do that! How in the world? This means stop cursing. I don't like to read the Bible because I don't understand half of what I read!"

I did become a mother to Susan's children in 1992 and 1993. I did become that preacher. I preached my first sermon in 1996, even though the pastor didn't believe in women preaching at all—absolutely not! God heard my cry one Saturday night. On Sunday morning, I shared with my pastor what God had spoken to me. Then my pastor said he'd had a dream, and in that dream, God showed him a lady coming into his office saying that God had called her to preach. The pastor cried and said, "I can't fight this anymore."

Why Me, Lord?

Maybe I was just the perfect candidate for the mission. I was chosen and handpicked by God.

For some reason, I came from a dysfunctional home. My mother had ten children. She knew how to survive, how to be a tough and strong woman. She was tough and unyielding. My biological father was not in the home and did nothing for me. He was married with a family. The first stepfather left the home the year I was born, 1964.

One of my older brothers went down a bad path at an early age doing unlawful things to help my mother. As he became older, it never stopped but continued. He started stealing for himself, not our mom. As a result, he spent thirty-six years in prison. I made sure our sons visited the prison two or three times a year with me. I would tell them, "If you start stealing or doing any illegal things in life, this is where you will be." I would minister to them about prison while driving there and back.

Another brother, when he became a teenager (age thirteen and again at age seventeen), left home to be in New York with his dad.

One of my sisters cried all the time. "I would like to be with my daddy sometimes. Why doesn't he ever come around? I want my daddy in my life. It's not my fault. Why?" I said, "Girl, he is married just like my daddy is. Our fathers have their families, and they don't care about you or me. Stop that crying. We can make it. One day we will not be in this house with our stepdad and our mother. We will be grown and have our own places. God will help us. I'm not gonna keep crying and missing a man who doesn't care about me. I'm gonna get me a salon one day and make me a whole lot of money, and I'm not gonna need him. He will look for me one day." And it happened just as I said. He started coming to my salon calling me daughter and crying about how sorry he was for not being a part of my life. I said, "No worries. I made it." But I was determined to make it with a good mind in spite of the situation. I made the best of it. Yes, God did help me. He supplied all my needs.

It could have been different. My mom tried hard to bring our stepdad close to us. He would say, "They are not my children. Find their daddy." Even though I was never close to my stepdad, I'm thankful my mother and stepdad took care of us. We never went without shoes, food, clothes, or other necessities. Our lights were never out, and we never had an eviction notice hanging on the front door. Our mom and stepdad had their house built in 1970. I still remember going by some days to see if it was finished or what had been done recently. I can still see the joy that was in their eyes because of their great accomplishment.

New Church

We had to leave our first church in the midst of my battle with Susan. We didn't leave because we didn't love the people there; we loved them dearly. I sang in the children's choir when I was between the ages of seven and twelve. Then I sang in the teen choir. Finally I sang in the mass choir until I was thirty-two.

My battle was a hard one with my husband's ex. I believe if I had stayed there, I would have lost the battle of saving our sons. I would have hurt myself and many others, and I would have disobeyed God. Why? The scriptures weren't pulled out so I could use them for spiritual warfare. The stories were preached very well, and I enjoyed church all through my beginning years. But after I married Abraham, God was telling me to be a mother to his sons. We did get custody of them while we were at that church, but all the time we were going through that process, I was cursing, angry all the time. When I did altar calls with very pretty prayers I had written out, I was a fake, a pretender. I was imitating the male preachers I had heard growing up at the church, so I knew how to do it well, but inside I had no real relationship with God.

I felt as if I was dying. That is the honest truth! I prayed, "Lord, if you send me to a pastor who can help me learn the Bible, so I can live a Godly life—a Zoe life—I will listen, and I will learn." I felt so bad because I knew I was not holy at all. I was a mess—an ugly mess.

It's On

Wow, what did I say that for? Abraham and I started visiting other ministries. We had no Word from God, no dream. We were not feeling a pull to any of them. Abraham said, "Let's put some names of churches in a box." I said, "Okay. I'm following you." Abraham put the names in a box and then pulled out the New Direction Church.

We started going to that church. Lord have mercy! That Word was cutting me so sharp, I was crying, convicted every Sunday, on the floor boo-hooing, angry, and misunderstood. I said, "Why did we have to come to this church? I don't like it. I don't like the pastor! He's always saying, 'Ain't no flesh going to be glorified in here. Worship, worship, worship the Lord!'" I said, "Who is he talking about? What is 'no flesh glorified'?" I said, "It's not me!" Lord, it was me. I was the main one, saying, "My makeup is on cute today. My hair is cute today! I'm not going to cry today. I'm not gonna be on the floor today screaming." But I did it again. I was on the floor screaming, "Lord, help me please!" I did that until I changed.

I changed, and I learned to love worship. I can't live without being in the presence of God daily.

Before I was filled with the Holy Ghost, I was taking a vitamin for stress, called It's Your Life. I didn't need the vitamin; I needed Jesus and to be filled with the power of the Holy Ghost.

Thank God for deliverance for Sarah. I was saved, too, from hell and prison of the traps of the enemy. Wow! God has a way of doing things! We're not smart enough to figure out all God is doing through us and for us.

God is all powerful. He is omnipotent. He has infinite power

He is omnipresent. God is present everywhere at the same time.

God is intimately related to *all* things and has access to *all* of reality.

The bottom line was that I just had to die to my own flesh. I was worse than all of them. I was just chosen for this mission. John 12:24–25 says, "Verily, verily I say unto you. Except a corn of wheat fall into the ground and die, it abideth alone: but if it dies it bringeth forth much fruit. He that loveth his life shall loose it, and he that hateth his life in this world shall keep it unto life eternal" (KJV).

I finally was being filled with the Holy Ghost. All through 1998, 1999, and 2000, I was growing in the Word, changing my thoughts and mind and words to be like Christ.

Romans 12:1: "Therefore, I urge you, brothers and sisters, in view of God's Mercy to offer your bodies as a living sacrifice, holy and pleasing to God; this is your true and proper worship" (KJV). This is one of our leading scriptures. It is one that our apostles have preached upon for many years.

My Sister-in-Law

I tried to get out of this situation. I really did. I asked my sister-in-law to get custody of the children. My flesh was warring with my spirit. My spirit said yes. My flesh said no; it's too much work. My flesh wanted to work and make money and enjoy life—go on cruises, buy new cars, travel the world, go to church (for sure) and sow seeds, pay tithes.

I said to my sister-in-law, "Abraham and I are doing very well financially. We can pay you to take care of these children."

I realized later that for someone to live somebody else has to die. I had to die to my will, die to my flesh so that my husband and the kids could live and I could be saved from the prison of hell. I gave up and accepted the challenge. My sister-in-law wouldn't do it. Susan kept doing her thing. I looked at the situation. I analyzed the whole thing in the natural and in the Spirit, and God was saying, "It's you, Sarah. This is your purpose; this is your mission.

Sacrifices had to Be Made

If God places you in a blended family or you marry a person who has children, those children have to be supported. A sacrifice is a loss or something you give up, usually for the sake of a better cause. Parents sacrifice time and money and sometimes sleep to take care of their children. In the beginning of a marriage, the money sometimes overflows and sometimes underflows. Whichever it is, it will change after a period of time. Ours started out with an overflow for seven years. For the next seven years, we had an underflow. During our underflow years, there were things I sometimes needed or wanted. I didn't have the extra money at the time to get what I wanted. I began to pray about it, talking to God. I said, "You are my provider. I am a tither. I've obeyed your Word. I'm expecting you to supply all my needs." And, yes, after I prayed, the need would be met. I had to wait and sacrifice some of my own wants because what our sons needed had to be first. Yes, I cried. I didn't like it. But God said, "I'm testing your heart to know what's in it" (Deuteronomy 8:2). He already knows what's in every man's heart. The testing reveals to us the quality of our faith before God. Will we trust God when we have lots of money in our bank accounts? Will we trust God when we feel we don't have enough money in our bank accounts? 1 John 3:20: "God knows all things" (NIV). Do not faint, do not walk away. Get tough and unyielding. Fight and keep moving. Continue in love. Galatians 6:9 says, "And let us not be weary in well doing for in due season we shall reap, if we faint not" (KJV). I have quoted that scripture so many times, but it came to pass. Be committed to the end, my sister, my brother. We win in God!

This Book is Not Meant to Hurt Anyone

This is my story. It recounts what happened to me over twenty years ago. I believe God wants me to share my story so that many lives can be changed and many children can be saved. And I pray that many will move in love and compassion and in the power of God. I pray that coparents will get along better for the kingdom. Please put God first; everyone else in the circle will be blessed as they see things differently—not my way, but God's way through his Word.

We all are wiser now, older and more mature. We have put childish things behind us. Susan is a new person; we live in peace and love. We love all the sons and love all our grandchildren.

Let's make this world a better place. Know this: We all have issues; let's work on them to be better than we were yesterday. 1 Peter 5:10: "God will restore, confirm, strengthen and establish you" (ESV).

My Story Behind the Glory

We all have a story, a lifelong dream. We endure hardship like a good sailor. We know the direction of the finish line. There's a process.

You don't look like what you've been through. Do not despise your humble beginning. Don't compete with anyone; rather, complete your mission—yes, your mission.

> Psalm 118:17: "I shall not die but live and see the salvation of the Lord" (KJV).

CHAPTER 3

———◆———

Abraham's Story

Abraham's mother, Mrs. Mae Wilkerson, is loving and kind; she is very sweet to each of her children. She has the spirit of a lamb and will sacrifice to provide for others. She has never been the cursing type, even in the fire of opposition. She is the mother of six children; Abraham is her fifth child. Our three sons once lived with her in 1989. She's a wonderful mom and an awesome grandmother today.

My mother-in-law did not agree with us getting custody of the children. She said the children were not my concern. She felt this was not my battle to fight. She would just say, "Let it happen." She was not able to see the things God had showed me and told me. I'm sure she just wanted all the noise to stop.

Abraham Is a Man of Many Gifts—God Blessed His Mind and Hands

I can say so much about my husband and never say it all. I have been with Abraham for twenty-nine years now, and so much has taken place. I have watched this man of God make a complete turnaround. Abraham not only can make, build, and fix anything, this great man of God is an excellent Bible teacher. He will have you laughing so hard with his own style and personality. When Abraham finishes teaching, you will say, "Oh my! Only he would think to put it like that. That was a great point he made. I got it!"

When I first met Abraham, his mom would say, "We just call Abraham. He can fix anything."

After Abraham came off the road from driving the eighteen-wheeler, he began working at our church during the day. Along with other staff members, he did various remodeling jobs and some administrative assignments.

During the evenings, he worked on cars, foreign and domestic. He put motors in cars and took them out. Abraham had taken some classes at a technical school one season while he worked at Toyota and Mazda dealership. That was a blessing! He sold large barbeque pit grills to many families. Years later he sold replicas of the Ark of the Covenant (the same size as the one in the Bible) to many churches. Abraham knew how to make money; he was determined to provide for his family. That was his number-one priority. After some years passed, he began to work for a module home company along with our sons. By the time they were old enough to work, Abraham trained them, and they were able to earn money for themselves.

One year my air conditioner unit went out at the salon. I didn't have the money to purchase a new one. Abraham said to me, "I have an idea." I said, "What do you have in mind?" He said, "I can take the unit from the building that was given to us for Winners Medallions." I said, "You can do that?" He did it. It was a miracle. I said, "Lord have mercy. You always making a way for us." My landlord hadn't cared either way—we could fix the problem or move out.

One evening I came home from the salon a little early. My husband had stripped a Mercedes Benz down, and parts were laying everywhere. I got so scared. I said, "Baby, what's going on? Why are all these car parts all over the yard? And whose nice car is this?" He looked at me and said, "Don't worry your pretty little heart. I got this." Then he told me whose car it was. I got scared again. I said, "Man, you are not from Nashville. You don't know the people here like I do. This guy will kill you! He's my cousin, but he is known for having people killed if they mess him around. Did you know that?" With the grace of God, they became very good friends. He gave Abraham another Mercedes to take apart, and the trust had begun. They continued to do business together for many years.

In most circumstances, Abraham is an introvert—meaning he would rather be alone minding his own business and watching one of his favorite TV shows. Abraham has zero tolerance for drama. He is not a weak man at all, he has great strengths and is able to help me in the areas were I was weak. Abraham served in the US military. He was in the Army and National Guard for eight years. He learned to handle all kinds of weapons, but he was not a violent man. He carried a pistol—a .38 to be exact.

I am definitely not trying to portray him as being weak. I'm just telling my story and what I saw and heard in the beginning stages of my marriage and my assignment and mission.

This is what my husband has to say about the matter:

> I was not afraid or timid. I've seen situations in which a husband gets put in jail for losing control. I didn't want to go to jail for assaulting my ex. I've seen some relatives who were involved in many fightings and confrontations. My mother was a very quiet and reserved person. She didn't do a lot of verbal teaching, but I watched her actions and her lifestyle. I received a lot of her mannerisms. In heated situations, she would not overreact to the problem. She would get on her sewing machine and start sewing just as if other people were not saying anything to her.

> My father would talk loudly and say things that were very hurtful. He'd make promises to our family that he never kept. He was absent eighty percent of the time. I never heard my mother ever use a curse word, no matter what the circumstance or challenge was, even in disappointment. For example, when school started, she would ask for a certain amount of money that we needed. My father would show up with half of what she had asked for. At Christmas time, he did the same thing—show up with half of what she had asked for. He was a man who was very difficult to deal with and hard to reason with.

He was the kind of father who would say, "My way or the highway." So I decided to not walk in any of his ways. My father was a heavy drinker of alcohol and still loves it today.

We were twenty-five years old, very young and immature, when we met. The only difference between us was that I knew how to fight and didn't mind doing it. I'd get my enemies off me and was determined not to live in confusion. The men's ministry at New Direction helped Abraham so much. It changed my husband into a strong giant. He grew into a great man of God.

I told my husband, "I hate confusion. I hate drama." So we have never ever had a fight. We may disagree about some things, but as time passed, we reasoned together. Love always won and kept us together, walking in Christ, following His method of operation. I love my husband, and I know his heart.

My husband hates fighting. He knows how to fight; he was a military man. He is very intelligent and can do anything better than most men.

I was determined to get victory. At first, I knew probably only two or three scriptures. "They were faith is the substance of things hoped for the evidence of things not seen" (Hebrews 11:1 KJV). Don't be a God robber (Malachi 3:8).

I started paying tithes as a teenager, and I never stopped.

"Write the vision, and make it plain" (Habakkuk 2:2 KJV). I heard this a lot in the church we attended in the first seven years of our marriage.

Yes, we were immature at the beginning of our marriage, especially when it came to reading and learning the Word, praying all through the day, and meditating on the Word. No, we did none of that. I was not getting up early seeking the face of God. We were young and loved each other and wanted to enjoy each other. Abraham and I wanted to enjoy the blessing of Abraham—good health, good success, long life, and prosperity. I also wanted to start a business, and yes, I did with the help of my husband. My salon opened in October 1990.

Once we got some order, we moved our sons in with us. We kept serving the Lord, studying the Word, letting the Spirit guide us. It's been amazing. Our God is awesome, and we love Him.

Abraham changed an automatic transmission over to a five-speed to keep from saying no to Susan. I saw the pictures of the car parts. I said, "What's this about?" He said, "I changed my Jetta Volkswagen over to a five-speed." I said, "Why?" He said, "So Susan couldn't drive it." I said, "Why didn't you just say no?" He said he didn't want to hurt her feelings. He also said she was riding guys around in his car.

Abraham and I Never Agreed on Fighting

Abraham told our sons not to fight at school or they would get a paddling at home after school if they did. Abraham said, "My mother didn't teach us to fight. She said tell the teacher."

I said, "Take the paddling. At least you won't grow up scared and always afraid to fight back, running in fear. Children will laugh at you, mistreat you, disrespect you, and bully you. Fight!"

My mother made us fight, after school, some kids beat my sister and I up. After sharing with our mother what happen, she knew we didn't win the fight. She took us back to the fight and said, "Get out of this car and fight!", my mother was not going to have it said that we lost the fight. I told our boys, "Kids will bully you if you don't fight back." My husband and I never agreed on fighting back. One son said, "Why can't you and Daddy reach one accord about fighting?" I said, "Son, you choose. We were raised differently. I'm sorry. Fight back or get bullied at school. It's your choice. Take your paddling from your daddy when you get home from school. You choose."

What's It's For

One year, my husband decided our sons had outgrown the spankings, so he made a paddle and named it "What's It's For." When they did something wrong and they needed more than a talking to, Abraham would pull out the What's It's For. After each lick, they had to explain why they were getting a paddling. This discipline worked. They did not get many paddlings. Just to see the rod of correction sitting in the corner was a good reason to do what was right. My mother always said, "If you refuse to discipline your children, they will embarrass you and make you ashamed one day." <u>Proverbs 29:15 KJV: "The rod and reproof give wisdom: but a child left to himself bringeth his mother to shame."</u>

Abraham said, "Let's just move away from Nashville."

My husband wanted to move away to Florida. He had met a guy who had an uncle who owned a trucking company. Abraham could drive for him. I said, "No, we can't. I want to stay here where all my clientele are." I was not gonna run from Susan. Of course I could have built a new clientele anywhere. I had been trained in beauty school in how to build a clientele anywhere, and I did it in Memphis, Tennessee. I did at Salon 102, and I did at Salon 808.

I knew I had to do what God was speaking to me about the boys. Neither Abraham nor anyone else believed me at first when I kept saying, "God is speaking to me in prayer and in dreams. He is saying, 'Be a mother to these children. Stop calling them your stepchildren when you pray. I will give them to you." It was hard for me to believe it sometimes myself. At that time, we could not leave the city of Nashville, Tennessee. When I would tell people, they would just look at me as if to say, "Really?" Yes, God communicates with those who seek his face.

CHAPTER 4

My Mother

Mrs. Rachel Kirkland—The Lion

My mother, an incredible lady had the spirit of a lion, taught me how to be tough, bold, and strong. She taught me how to win, and even how to be confrontational and stand in the mist of opposition. She would say "trouble is easy to get in and hard to get out of, have the wisdom to know when to walk away from some situations. God didn't give me a spirit of fear. God did give us power, love, and sound minds so we can move forward. At the time, I thought my mother was molding me to be a mean and hateful person. I didn't realize the truth until I had to deal with people who just weren't nice, people who tried to put fear in me, people who loved to fight and curse me to make me do what they wanted me to do. When I matured in the Lord, I said, "Wow! Jesus was both a lamb and a lion. My mother meant for me to be fierce in the natural; I learned later to be fierce as a lion in the Spirit realm for Christ.

I thank God for my mother. She taught me how to fight and how to go to war. I turned it around. I learned to do it in the Spirit. Now I fight in the Spirit and I know how to *win! I refuse to live intimidated and defeated by the devil.*

That was my mother, Mrs. Rachel Kirkland. She is deceased now. Thank you, Mama!

My mother was an excellent cook. Early in the morning—around 4:30 or 5:00—I sometimes got up to go to the bathroom. I would hear her in the kitchen—pots would be boiling, and she'd be frying meat in a hot skillet. The food smelled good! I'd think, *What is she doing up so early in the kitchen?* It was important to her that we eat breakfast before school and supper when we got home from school. My brother Ronald cooked the cornbread after school; he was the oldest of the five who were at home. My mom had her first set of five children; then later she had a second set of five children. One sister lived with grandma in Wheeler, on the Bird Place.

When we were little, my mother drove us to school and picked us up from school. Later, when we were older, we rode the school bus. She worked while we were in school. My mother always worked, and her husband always worked. I always saw them pay their own bills; never did I see or hear them cursing or demanding others to do for them or bully other people to do this for them, do that for them. She said often they paid their own light bills. "Work for what you want in life," she said, "and if you are broke, never tell anyone. Nobody knows how much money you have until you open your mouth and tell them. If you don't have it, wait till you get it." I learned good work ethics from my mother. My mother passed at sixty-eight years old. I dreamed it before it happened. I woke up with tears in my eyes. I woke up my husband and I said, "I've been crying at my mother's funeral." He said, "What?" I was the only one who dreamed of my mother's passing. I asked my brothers and sisters if God had shown them anything, and everyone said no. God spoke to me and said, "Do all you can for her now because it won't be long." A year and a half later, she was gone. I bought her things and took her out to eat. We spent time together talking about God. I gave her some biblical teachings to listen to by T. D. Jakes and Rod Parsley. She would give me looks like, "She knows something." I did know something. God had shown me what was soon to be. Thank you, God, for showing me things to come. What an awesome God You are!

My Mother Moved Me from Chattanooga

My brother Paul told me that he drove to Chattanooga, picked me up, and brought me back to Alabama when I was seven years old. I went back during the summer to visit my Aunt Naomi (whom I called Big Momma) and her husband, my uncle, Big Daddy. All my Atlanta family was so sad that Baby Sarah had to leave to go back to Alabama to live with her mother. My aunt had taught me to be sweet, kind, loving. Basically, she taught me to be good to people and to get on my knees and pray and seek God. I can remember, just as if it was yesterday, Aunt Naomi down on her knees crying out to God. Even though I didn't understand, I would get down on my little knees and cry too.

My mother said to me, "You cry too much. I got to train you to stop all that crying. You are short, small, and a crybaby. I don't want you to be like my sister Naomi and my mother, Ruth. They were short and small too, and men fought them. I don't want you to let any man fight you and beat you up. No man or woman. Some women will mistreat you just because they don't like you, for no reason. I got to make you tough. If someone mistreats you, get them off you. Go home and cry. Handle your business." My mother would go toe to toe with anyone who tried to mistreat her.

When she disciplined us, sometimes she would say things like, "I'll put my fist in your mouth." I would say, "What did she say?" She was mean. (She never did that, however.) Lord have mercy! I was so scared. I told my Aunt Naomi how she was talking and handling us. My aunt said, "Baby, your mother would handle our daddy like he was a stuffed animal. She will kill you, baby. Don't make her mad." One time my ex said, "I will take my fist and go up side your head." I said, "Okay, and when you do, I will pick up this chair and hit you over your head!" I was not afraid. He unfolded his hand and said, "Sarah, will you hit me with that chair?" I said, "Yes. Yes, I will."

God used my mom to prepare me to fight back and not fear any man.

My mother did her best at teaching me to win the carnal way. She didn't know about winning in the Spirit. She knew I needed Jesus and should serve him in my life, but she didn't understand that we can win in Him; she didn't fully understand what it meant to be born again. My momma said, "Win the fight, no matter what it takes—fist, bat, stick, gun, and cursing." However, she loved God. But no one was going to run over her or her children. Mother didn't play like that.

One day my sister Shaneese and I were in a fight after school. When our mother picked us up, we told her about the fight. She said, "Did y'all win?" I looked at Shaneese. She looked at me. We both looked as if we were not sure. She said, "*!%!?#!* *no!* You didn't win! I'm taking you back!" When we got back to the school, she said, "Get out of this car and fight!" We got out of the car and did just what she said. The fight was on! She just stood there and looked. After it was all over, she said, "Now you've won. Get back in the car. Now we can go home." She kept saying, "You are supposed to win the *!%!?#!* fight! Anybody hit you, you kick their *!%!?#!*." She said, "Never start a fight. Let others be the ones bold enough to hit you first. All the other kids will get the message not to mess with you sisters."

Thanks to My Deceased Mother; my Stepfather, Willie Quincy; my Aunt Naomi (Big Momma); and my Uncle L.G. Haley (Big Daddy)

My mother, the strong fighter and survivor, taught me how to fight and win in all my natural situations. The lady could take a little of nothing and make the best meal; she was a wonderful cook. She tried hard to teach me not to be a crybaby. Every time things don't go as I expected, although, in Christ, I'm still a crybaby, I am strong in God, and still can and will get my enemies off me.

Stepdad Willie Quincy was a great provider. He made sure the bills were paid at all times.

My Aunt Naomi and Big Daddy came to Alabama and took me back to Chattanooga when I was in a baby walker. I believe it was the will of God. Although they had their card games and alcohol beverages, I was always in another room playing with my dolls and toys, being protected from their lifestyle. They had their fights, but I was in another room. I heard a little, but they never let me see it. My aunt loved praying and having a good time. She would tell me, "Get on your knees, and let's pray."

She prayed and cried. I did the same thing right beside her. I felt a lot of love and protection from Big Momma and Big Daddy. Thanks a million!

Big Daddy was a father to me when I was between one and six years old. I'm so thankful for the great times I spent with him and all my Atlanta family—my cousins, Lisa, Jill, and Thomas, and their wonderful mom, Betty, who drove me and my Aunt Naomi everywhere. My cousin Betty lived a glamorous and prosperous life. During my teen years, I struggled with hurt and pain, but what helped and give me hope was the fact that I could always reflect back at my life that I had lived as a child. That foundation really did help me; it made me smile and say "I can make it."

I thank God for my mother, my aunt, my grandma, and my God. They all helped me to be ready. I love people, I love righteousness, and I love order. I know how to be a lion and how to be a lamb. I know how to say I'm sorry when I'm wrong, I know how to repent and pray to my God when I make a mess of things. I know how to get before the Lord for any situation when I need help or a breakthrough. I open my Bible, read, listen and seek God.

Characteristics

Lion of Judah

Jesus is referred to as the Lion of Judah in Genesis 49:8–9.

The Lion of Judah, a strong fighter against the enemy, taking vengeance on His enemies. Jesus is believed to be a descendant of the Tribe of Judah. He is commonly referred to as the Overcoming One and the one qualified to open the Scrolls and Seven Seals. I am an overcomer.

Revelation 5:5 refers to Jesus as the Lion of Judah. The Lord Jesus is coming to judge the world as the Lion of Judah. We are overcomers; we have the Lion of Judah.

Lamb

Revelation 12:11 tells us: "And they overcame Him because of the blood of the Lamb" (NAS).

Jesus, the Lamb of God, was our once-and-for-all sacrifice that fulfilled God's need for a blood offering. He was the perfect sacrifice of love that brought the possibility of perpetual change to the world.

The law of Moses was unable to save us because of the weakness of our sinful nature. So God did what the law could not do. He sent His own Son in a body like the bodies we sinners have. And in that body, God declared an end to sin's control over us by giving his son as a sacrifice for our sins. Reference Romans 8:3.

We don't have to walk in our sinful nature. We have the Lamb of God.

The Scripture says, "Be angry but sin not" (Ephesians 4:26 NIV). We all still get made, saved or not saved. When people make me mad, I say, "Which one do you want—the Lamb or the Lion? My Aunt Naomi or my mother? Leave me alone.

Why Was My Mother Not in Agreement with Us Getting the Children?

She had lived longer than I, so she had seen that, after a person raises up another woman's children, some or most go back to the biological mother, the one who mistreated them. My mother called me a fool; she said I was wasting my time. She also believed the children would mistreat me when they became older. She felt the money I would use to raise them could be used for something else. I said, "All that matters, Mom, is that I obey God. He will never let us run low on money. I'm not worried about money."

I have learned that, when God gives you an assignment, He shows it to you, not to everybody else. I was called crazy names. I did a lot of crying, but God strengthened me even more. I still had the tenacity to keep moving forward in the will and purpose of God. I constantly kept saying, "Over my dead body will my husband's children be destroyed!"

This mission became my baby. I meant it. I was going to stand before my God and hear Him say, "Sarah, good and faithful servant, you have been faithful over a few things. Welcome home, my child. Well done, Sarah!"

The Lamb and the Lion

My mother was strong and tough and taught me to overcome. I chose to overcome through Christ, the Lion of Judah. God decides His will for us. We follow God's plan and His will; that is, if we will listen to Him. "He who has an ear, let him hear what the Spirit says to the churches" (Revelation 3:22 NKJV). I heard Him!

My Aunt Naomi sacrificed to help me. She taught me to pray and walk in the Spirit, not the sinful nature.

My Momma said, "You can buy Susan a Cadillac and put a big red bow on the front of it, and she still is not gonna like you. Stop helping her with her kids. She doesn't like you, and she doesn't appreciate you." I said, "I don't care, Momma. I'm doing what God said to do." She said, "What about what I said? I'm your mother." I said, "Momma, I have to obey God over you."

It just didn't make sense to my mother. She just didn't understand. God was making me strong in Him. I don't care if a person hates me. I still won't stop doing what is right by the boys, and people can't intimidate me. I see the vision, and I'm focused. No one can see what God is showing you. I'm seeing my future, and it looks better than my life is right now.

My mother told several people in the city of Nashville, "My daughter is a fool and acts like she has lost her mind!" Jesus did his Father's will, so can I do my Father's will.

Why did my mother have to be so tough, so strong, and so aggressive? Why would she quick to fight anyone that messed with her?

After I grew up and became a young lady, I began to think about all the things that I had heard about my family. I then realized what had happened. My mother's father, Lawson Fenoil, would fight her mother, Ruth Grace, all the time. I was told that my grandmother stayed under the house hiding from my grandfather; in fact, she stayed more there than she did in the house. I was told also that my mother's brother, who is my

Aunt Naomi's twin brother, Jack, was killed by my grandfather because he would defend my grandmother when he would see my grandfather fighting his mother. My mother also did the same thing. I was told that, as big and tall as my grandfather was, my mother would pick him up and pin him to the wall like a teddy bear and make him stop fighting her mother. My mother had to handle her own dad. I couldn't believe what I heard. My granddaddy never would fight my mother, but he killed Jack, his own son. My mother was the baby of the five siblings. (Yes, babies do get away with things that other siblings can't.) I knew my granddaddy, but I never met his wife, my grandmother, Ruth Grace. Granddaddy did go to prison as a result of shooting his son. I was told my grandmother fell out and died when he got out of prison. Nine years he stayed in prison. I never met my Uncle Jack either. These situations happened in 1952.

Our Stepfather

Although I do not like the word *step*, our stepfather wanted to be called stepdad. Quincy was his name, and he was not a strong man of the faith. For many years, he stayed at home on Sundays when we went to church with our mom. He felt that it was not important. In his later years—about ten years before he passed away he got saved and became a faithful flower of Christ—he started going to church and learning the Word.

Quincy was a kind man who loved us and provided for his household, making sure bills were paid. He loved his two stepdaughters and wanted the best for them. He was the kind of man who played it safe. He knew he wasn't our biological father, so he stepped back. I would hear him say to my mom, "Those are not my children." My mother would say, "Whip them if they act bad." He would say, "Oh no. Find their dads. Let them whip them." He didn't want any trouble from my dad or my sister's dad. Although they were not concerned about us, I would have loved it if he had treated us as if we were his children. Everyone does things differently, and maybe he didn't realize that it was necessary for us to have a father at home to teach us and explain to us about life, to prepare us for dating and marriage and things that a girl needs to know as a teenager from a man's perspective. He just would not play that role. He was a nice, quiet man in the home with us. When I was old enough to get a job after school, he would pick me up some nights. As we rode all the way home, he wouldn't say much of anything. After our mom passed, Shaneese and I cooked many dinners for him. He would smile and say, "Thank you." I could look in his eyes and see that he wished things could have been different in our relationship. We did grow up and bless him. The enemy had him thinking, *Don't do too much for them. They are not yours. They won't appreciate you when you get old. You'll see.* These were lies. The devil is the father of lies; he is the trap setter.

Our stepfather offered to pay me for the food I cooked for him. I said, "Quincy, I always cook too much. It's hard to cook a little because I'm used to cooking for four sons, Abraham, and me." I would say, "You don't owe me anything. I'm glad to be a blessing to you." Our mother cooked for him every day. I know he missed her and the meals she provided two to three times a day. She loved cooking lots of food. Our kindness amazed him, made him happy and he was very appreciative. *Those two girls grew up and now they are bringing me food.*

One time, years ago during my busy salon days, prosperous years, I visited my mother and step-farther for an hour or so before my next appointment. I will never forget what he said as he stared at a small white clock, "I wish I could turn back the hands of time. I would do some things different." I kept saying, "Oh, don't worry about those days. They're gone now." That particular day, I stopped by their house, and brought them a catfish plate and a monetary seed. They loved the fish from McCullum Catfish Restaurant. I was good to them when I had money; I would share even though they didn't ask. I'm a giver. I believe we as adults should give to your parents; they gave to us. My mother used to say, "Be good to people because you never know who may grow up and have to give you a glass of water." She had a lot of great nuggets of wisdom. I learned how to receive because of certain things she said. I listened to her more than she knew I did. I kept some things in my heart that she said.

My mother really wanted me to fight Susan, my husband's ex, or do something to make her leave me alone. It was always some kind of drama on a daily basis. The drama went on for years; I thought it would never end. I said, "Momma, I can't. The Holy Spirit doesn't want me to act that way." I was changing. She said, "You got my blood in you. You get her off you." I said, "I will. I know how through God. I have fought long enough in the flesh. No good thing dwells in the flesh. I've got to be like Jesus now. I know better. I can't win in the flesh, but I can win in the Spirit. What will please my God? He will fight for me. All I have to do is tell Him all about it. Momma, don't worry about me winning. You trained me to win with weapons of the flesh. God is training me His way with the weapons of the Spirit. I will win. Victory is in my veins."

My Mother's Point of View

I do understand why my mother was so upset. She had a daughter who had her own salon that was a prosperous business during those years, and now here she was taking care of four little boys, and then later their sister, who moved in and stayed a short time, now a total of five children.

I looked at her point of view. She was born on March 13, 1933. She quit school in the third grade to pick cotton in the fields to help her parents. She was the mother of ten children. From 1963 to 1964 she cooked at the Greater Country Club restaurant, washed cars, sold liquor and beer to take care of her children.

I'm sure my mother thought, *This child of mine could be doing something else with her money instead of taking care of another woman's children.* My mom was not lacking anything, she just hated the idea that I was spending my money on another woman's children. She was also angry at the ex, Susan, because she knew how ugly Susan had been to me. She never understood my situation. I was on a mission for the Lord. I had to be obedient to God. Acts 5:29 tells us, "It's better to obey God than to obey man" (KJV).

My mother knew that Susan was so ungrateful and unappreciative of the blessing. Again, I had to obey God rather than obey man.

CHAPTER 5

———•———

Mrs. Naomi Grace- The Lamb

My Aunt Naomi—we called her Big Momma— lived in Chattanooga, Tennessee. She taught me to be loving, sweet, sacrificial, and humble like the Lamb of God.

My mother gave me to my aunt when I was about six months old and we were living in the projects. I was in a baby walker. My Aunt Naomi cried a lot. I didn't know why at first, but I found out later in life. Her father, my granddaddy, killed her twin brother and went to prison for it in 1952. I guess that's why I cried so much too. In spite of her pain, she and her husband, L. G. Haley, and her daughter, Betty, took very good care of me. She encouraged me to continue to love and give myself away to my mission. She always said, "Love those children and trust God in your situation or leave it alone, because God wants you to be good to them. God will get you for mistreating those little children." She would say, "Do you hear me, little girl? God will have rubies and diamonds in heaven waiting for you." I would hold the phone and cry, saying, "Okay, I will." My Aunt Naomi Haley is deceased now. Yes, she made many sacrifices for me, and I thank God for this lady. She loved me as if I was her own child.

We went to church every Sunday, just us two. Someone would drop us off, or we would take a taxicab. She shouted all the time; chairs were always flying. I would cry; I hated it. I thought people were throwing chairs at her. I was too young to understand why she cried; I would cry too. I can

35

still see it. I said to myself, *I don't like this place. Every time we come here, they throw chairs at my Big Momma.* I just really could never see who was throwing the chairs. She would be shouting, and others would be shouting. Church was noisy, and chairs were moving. I would be crying. I loved my Big Momma, and I didn't know who was making her cry. Then I thought someone was hitting her to make her cry. When I became older, I finally figured it all out: it was all the work of the Holy Ghost in the people(at least I hope so). I was told that my granddaddy would go to the church when they were kids and beat them out of the church, saying, "Go home!" I guess she was so glad to be free to go to church and praise the Lord.

One summer while I was living in Chattanooga, my granddaddy came to live with us after he was released from prison. He said, "I'll buy Sarah school clothes this year. Will three hundred dollars be enough?" I can still hear my cousin Betty. She said, "Three hundred dollars is not enough to get Sarah school clothes." I said to myself, *Isn't three hundred dollars a lot of money?* This happened in 1973 or 1974. I thought, *Maybe it's not a lot for Cousin Betty. She really likes nice things.* She shopped at exclusive department stores such as Loveman's department store in Chattanooga. I can remember being at the top of the escalators when I was very young. When we would go shopping, I was so afraid to move; they would pick me up and carry me down.

I believe God moved me to Chattanooga, Tennessee, when I was a toddler in 1965 to live with my Aunt Naomi and Uncle L. G. Haley. I believe God's hand was up on me. He brought me out and placed me in a different environment with my Aunt Naomi and Uncle L. G. so I could get the experience that I needed to help mold me and prepare me for a different and unusual purpose. My Aunt Naomi was a very compassionate woman, and because of her, I learned how to love and show compassion and sacrifice as they all did for me. My cousin Betty live an extravagant life. Her husband owned a night club. Money was plentiful, and they both had jobs. Some years she worked and some years she didn't. Cousin Betty drove us around in her Lincoln Continental. I sat right in the middle on the booster seat. There were no safe car seats for children back then. Federal standards for safe seats didn't come out until 1971.

My mother could have chosen any one of my siblings to send to Tennessee. I believe she were led by God, however unknowingly, to pick me. There are no mistakes or coincidences with God. He has a way of getting his purpose done. The seed was planted in me. Now, as an adult, I can easily give back what grew from that seed. I thank God for my beginning foundation; I believe it was divinely designed.

I can remember riding through downtown Chattanooga in the Lincoln. Betty would blow her horn—bump, bump—and wave like a royal queen. The people would say, "That's Big Melvin's wife, with her shades on and the wind blowing through her hair, looking lovely as always." We were looking good! James—aka Big Melvin—had three jobs. He had a day job, and in the early evenings, he ran the numbers (he was the Bookie Man). After seven in the evening, he ran his night club, which was called Mel's Place. Money was plentiful. I was called the Lucky Ticket Baby because I would pull a ticket off the book for their friends, and they would win money many times.

Aunt Naomi

For years, Aunt Naomi and her daughter, Cousin Betty, made sure that I had a birthday present in the mail every year until I was about fifteen or sixteen years old. Money would arrive in a card, or a box would arrive containing a beautiful outfit. I can remember the new clothes I received from Chattanooga by mail when I was in elementary school. My Cousin Betty bought very nice clothes for her two girls. After I moved back to Alabama, she would send a huge box of last year's clothes to all of us.

My cousins told me that I use to sit in my walker and sing, sing, sing all day. I couldn't talk, but could hum songs. Then when I did start singing, they said my favorite song was "Shotgun." The part I sang best was "I said, Shotgun! Shoot 'em 'fore they run now." The song was written by Junior Walker and performed by Junior Walker and the All Stars.

They said the next door neighbors would come over and say, "Where's that singing baby? Tell her to come out and sing us a song." My cousins said I'd come out singing "Shotgun." I was told that my oldest cousin said, "I wish she'd get another song to sing for the neighbors." My cousins said my head was like a juke box. My mother played RB music all day, and the album kept playing over and over again. My mother was selling whiskey and beer and kept her music playing, so I came out singing. My cousin said, "I'm tired of that one song. I know she knows other songs." When they would request me to sing, for some reason I sang "Shotgun." I guess I liked the beat—ha ha!!!

Visiting Alabama

Times have changed since 1969. Back then, children could ride the train by themselves. I can remember riding the train from Chattanooga to Alabama by myself. The first time my Aunt Naomi rode with me, and she said, "The next time, you will be traveling by yourself." She would tell me, "Don't be scared. The train attendants will be watching you. See that lady? And see that lady?" She pointed out the female attendants to me who would watch over me. She also told me that she would give the attendants money for my food.

In 1981, some of my brother Ronald's friends asked me if I remembered the conversation we'd had when I came home to visit my mom. I was only about five years old, and I couldn't remember what I had said to them. They made me remember. They said they would say, "Where have you been, Baby Sarah?" I would say, "I just got off the Chattanooga choo-choo!" I remembered after they reminded me. I also remembered the different workers on the train who watched over me until the train arrived in Alabama.

Living In Chattanooga

My family members loved to have a good time on the weekends with their friends. When I was in a room playing with all my toys and dolls, the door would be cracked, and sometimes I could see them drinking their beer and wine and playing cards. They would be laughing and cooking fish, hot dogs, slaw, and other favorites. Big Melvin, with his black briefcase, would stop by. Someone would say, "Go get Baby Sarah and let her pull a ticket for me." They wanted to win some money. People would pick me up and put me in their lap and say, "Pull the winning ticket for me! Which one do you think it is?" The tickets were attached to a long piece of paper; numbers were printed on each one.

I also remember my cousins taking me to the malls and other stores. They would take me on picnics in parks, at lakes, and in the mountains. They would also take me to their homes quite often. My Aunt Naomi was my cousin's grandmother. I had many birthday parties in Chattanooga. I would pass out my invitations in the neighborhood to all my friends.

I would go with my Uncle L. G. (Big Daddy), my Aunt Naomi's husband, to the barber shop and other places. He would put me on his shoulders and put me in the car, and we would ride until I fell asleep. I never experienced him touching me in the wrong way. Of course, he knew my mother, the lion, but I don't think he even thought like that. I spent many years with him and my Big Momma. All of those times have given me great and long-lasting wonderful memories that I will never forget.

My Aunt Naomi (Big Momma) didn't work outside the home; she was a stay-at-home mom. My Uncle L. G. (Big Daddy) worked at a steel plant in Chattanooga. A day with Big Momma went like this: We'd get up, and she would say, "Sarah, we're going to the store." We would walk to the side market store and pick up a few items. (My aunt couldn't drive). We would come back, and she would go in the kitchen to cook and start humming different songs and praying, "Yes, Lord!" She'd be crying and cooking. I never understood at that time why she cried so much and talked to the Lord so much. I did later in life. I would ask, "Can I go outside and play?" If she said it was okay, I would go out and play in the dirt making pretend food with grass, rocks, and dirt, putting it on plates as if it was something really good. Then I would get all my dolls and take them outside. I'd dress them in different outfits and shoes. If I didn't run out time, I ride my tricycle for a while. Finally Big Momma would call out to me and say, "It's time to eat!" After we sat down for a wonderful meal, it was time to get a bath, have my hair combed, and take a nap. I hated to come inside. I loved being outside playing in the sun. I hated getting my hair done. It hurt so bad because it's so thick and coarse. I would lie on her lap while she combed my hair, and I'd cry until I fell asleep. I loved this lady; she took very good care of me. Her favorite shows were *Bonanza* with Ben Cartwright (played by Lorne Greene) and *Gunsmoke* with Matt Dillon (played by James Arness). She would say, "Give it to 'em, Matt Dillon!"

My Aunt Crossing Over

God was taking her home, sending a band of angels to sing to her. She called me at my salon, and I could feel in my spirit it was her before I answered the phone. I hated to answer the phone. I just felt it was a death phone call, and I was right. I picked up, and she said, "I'm leaving here. The angels are here to take me home. If you want to see me again, come on before I leave here. I'm tired of this old body; I'm ready to go home. I hear angels singing." The next day, the boys and I loaded into our Quest van. I picked her up another TV and some food, and we drove to Chattanooga. I was praying: "God, please let her live a while longer." And she did. She lived about three or four weeks after that. When I made it to her house, she kept saying, "The angels are here. Don't you hear them singing?" I said, "No, I don't see them and I don't hear them." She said, "Well, they are here." She said, "Get my coat and my hat. I'm ready to go. I'm tired of this aching body. I'm gonna get a new heavenly body. These doctors want me to eat food I don't like. My daughter kept bringing me foods I don't want to eat." I was crying. I didn't want her to leave me. I realized it was her time. She was going the way we all will go one day; we leave this earth and go to be with the Lord.

Great Cooks

Big Momma loved me, and I loved her. I used to pick blackberries when I was a little girl. Well, I attempted to pick black berries. Big Momma would give me a bowl, and I would go outside. In no time at all, I would come back in with what I thought was enough black berries to make a pie. One time I said, "Big Momma, will you make me a pie?" She looked into the bowl and said, "Baby, you do not have enough berries to make a pie. It takes a lot of berries to make a pie." I said, "I'll go get some more." In a short while I came back in and said, "Is this enough?" She said, "No, baby, but it is enough to make you a blackberry dumpling!" I said, "Okay, I'll eat a blackberry dumpling!" She and my mother were excellent cooks. When they got together in the kitchen, I could hear each of them bragging about each other's cooking. "No, you cook this better than I do!" "No, you can cook that better than I do!" They both could make wonderful homemade biscuits and serve them with fried corn cut from the cob. Oh my God! All the family would show up to eat peach and blackberry preserves, fried pork chops, and fried chicken. It didn't matter where they were—in the kitchen in Chattanooga or in the kitchen in Alabama—when those two ladies got together, it was on in the kitchen! I miss those two ladies—my mother and my Aunt Naomi.

CHAPTER 6

———◆———

At Grandma's House During the Summer

This admirable, amazing lady is the one that all my mother's children called Grandma. Although she was the grandmother of only some of my siblings, she loved us all. Mrs. Ettoy Jakes had many children at her house. She was the grandmother of my mother's first husband's children. She loved all children, no matter who they were. We spent some weeks with her during the summertime. When I wasn't in Chattanooga, Tennessee, with my Aunt Naomi, I would go to the country. Our granddad, Mr. Willie Jakes of Wheeler, Alabama, kept a huge garden along with chickens, cows, pigs, and horses. And they had an outdoor toilet. We definitely lived off the land when we stayed with them. During the summer, we helped Grandma and Grandpa shell snap beans. Each of us had a bowl in our lap as we tried to do what Grandma was doing. When our mother would come to pick us up at the end of summer, Grandma would say, "Daughter, take this home for the children." She would give us blackberry jelly and peach jelly along with corn and greens in plastic bags. She'd give us frozen peas and beans and meats. My mother would say, "Mother, that's enough!" Grandma would keep going into the house to get more. She influenced me greatly because of her giving spirit.

I really felt loved a lot as a child, and I felt special. My childhood foundation was beautiful. I am so grateful for all of the wonderful memories and how each environment helped to make me the lady I am today. I never really thought about it until now—until I started writing this book. I believe that's why I love children so much. I cannot stand it when children are mistreated. I will always be a blessing to children.

For a while, I was the baby of them all. Five years later, my mother had two more girls. Yes, we did get whippings. Grandma whipped us sometimes. She would say, "Go outside and get me a switch!" We cried a little when it was over. She was very good to us, but she did not let us get out of line. There was no talking back or rolling of eyes. We obeyed, or a switch would be coming our way then, not later on. Having temper tantrums was not heard of.

I can remember going up in a helicopter with my cousin, Hoffman Kelly, Sr., to spray the fields with poison to kill the insects. Believe it or not, I was not afraid to go up in that small helicopter; I loved being high off the ground.

I can remember going to the outdoor toilet at grandmother's house. That was scary! Chickens was always in the path form the house to the outhouse. When it was bath time, my grandmother would boil water and put it into a number-ten tin tub. We would bathe three at a time. While we waited for our turn to get into the tub, we would get our little clothes out. I can remember my underwear, each one had a day of the week printed on them. You know that made me feel special. I also had a beautiful small blue suitcase that my Aunt Naomi purchased for me. My mother and my Chattanooga family purchased many nice things for me over the years. Even though all of the material things are long gone, the loving memories will last a lifetime.

Thank God for real grandmas, heaven sent to love
us all. My Grandma is deceased now.

CHAPTER 7

Children

The first time I saw the boys with Susan was in 1980 at a mailbox in the projects—the same projects where I was born. I was standing on the porch of my ex-boyfriend's uncle's apartment in the projects with a high school classmate. I said, "Girl, look. Are those twins?" She said, "Yes. The mom is nice. Go look at them. She'll let you." Suddenly it felt as if I had chains or something wrapped around my legs and ankles so I couldn't move off the porch. My friend pushed me, encouraging me to look. "What's wrong with you?" I said, "I can't." When she asked me why, I said, "I feel as if something is holding me back so I can't move." It was like a small voice that said, "Not now." So I did not move. That was in 1980. I met their father years later. He was in the army in 1980, which is why I never saw him then. The boys were four years old by then. I said to myself, *These are the same little boys I wanted to go look at years ago.* God wouldn't let me look at them then. Wow! God's ways and timing are perfect and right.

The First Day I Met the Three Boys
at Abraham's Mom's House

I said, "Oh my!" I looked in their eyes. I could see their low countenance and withdrawn expressions. Something was missing from their personalities. I said to myself, *I can help them. With much love and happiness, they will be smiling with joy and excitement.* I could see us at parks, swimming, laughing, and shopping for toys and other things they would like. I could picture cooking for them, cutting their hair, dressing them alike, talking with them, and taking them to church. So many things were crossing my mind. I really fell in love with them the first day we all spent together.

When Abraham and I started dating, all the boys attended elementary school. Six months later, Abraham asked me to marry him. I knew already we would be married. God had shown me that Abraham would be my husband. I said, "Yes, yes, yes!" We had a beautiful outdoor wedding. The boys were part of the wedding. Everything was lovely and beautiful. Many family members and friends came to celebrate our big day. The next day, when the boys went home, one boy told his mama they had a new "momma step." The drama started. Susan kept them away from us for a month or more. Half of the hell that we went through with Susan has not been told. The devil was using her to the utmost. It seemed as if it just wasn't going to ever stop. I had to make decisions. Should I stay in the relationship, or should I get out fast? The devil raised his head. First, my marriage had to be saved. Second, my man had to be encouraged (saved from Susan's traps, tricks, and lies) until one day she met Sarah. And third, the children had to be saved. My mind was moving ... decisions, decisions. I saw the battle, and I knew it would be long and hard. Do I stay? Do I leave? Do I fight? Do I run? Of course not! I will fight, and I will win. I could hear my mother's voice: "You win the fight! Run into it!"

The days, months, and the years went by. I spent my time praying, watching, and crying. We went through court case after court case: mess, mess, mess, drama, drama, drama. It just wouldn't stop. Some people you just can't help; they want what you have and more. They laugh, ignorantly thinking they are getting over on you, thinking you're stupid or you're the fool. My number-one priority was to save the children. My man and I were being saved through the process of Susan's traps. We finally did get an attorney, and the judge gave us custody of the children. It was a blessing to have them out of the noisy, chaotic environment that gave me a headache when I thought about it. Peace came for a little while until Satan saw where Susan could come in again. The children started elementary school.

Abraham and I built a great relationship with the staff and the principal of the school. Whatever they needed from us we gave it. I also gave them my salon phone number so they could call me anytime. I was there for PTA meetings and plays. (Abraham was on the road most times.) Yes, we were supportive for all five children.

On our way to school, we prayed in the car and we read a scripture. I would always keep Bibles in the car. Each day they would take turns reading a passage. One passage they read a lot was Proverbs 24:33: "A little sleep, a little slumber a little folding of the hands to rest and poverty will come on you like a thief and scarcity like a armed man." (NIV) They talk about the scriptures today, and they remember several of them.

The First Year that the Boys Lived with Us They Missed Susan So Much

The boys only talked about how they missed her at bedtime. I would tuck them in and read a bedtime story to them. Among other books, they loved *Over the Rainbow* by Judy Collins and E. Y. Harburg, and *Green Eggs and Ham* by Dr. Seuss. I would then pray with them.

My mother-in-law had some old pictures of Susan. She gave some to me, so at night I would put her picture under their pillows. What hurt them hurt me; I would do all I could to not let them see my cry. When one of them would say, "Momma Sarah, I miss my other momma," I would say, "Yes, baby, I know you do. I understand, and you will see her soon." We always kept order so Susan could see them. We set up a system, everyone got used to it, and after a period of time, the sadness did leave. The boys embraced their new lives with us. Sometimes they would say, "It's quiet over here. We like it." Our sons were good kids. Hardly ever did they have a babysitter. A few of my family members, a close friend of mine, and my mother-in-law sometimes helped out, but most times they were with me. I was very careful about who kept them; I constantly watched and prayed. I never wanted to hear twenty years later that a person did this or that to our boys. Oh, no! No. No way.

We Did Do a Lot of Praying

I used to tell the boys that the reason for prayer was to provide a protective shield to cover them when they left home. I knew one day they would leave home, so I prayed and prayed almost every day; we sometimes skipped a day or two. We would pray and cry and worship God. I also wanted them to experience the love and the presence of God at home. We laid a foundation of worshiping God. Sometimes my husband would lead us in prayer. My husband sometimes was in the backyard working as a mechanic to make some extra money to add to his check for bills. My husband would say, "Faith without works is dead. I'm the man of this house. I am responsible for making sure these bills are paid." My husband loves God and loves prayer, praise, and worship. He knew how much time he had to spend with us in prayer, and he also knew how much time he had to finish up working on the cars in the garage and in our backyard.

Childhood Is So Important: Parents, Protect Your Children from Evil Spirits

Evil spirits are traps of the enemy; evil spirits enter into a person's life when they are weak. The weakest time is childhood. Children are completely dependent on their parents or others for protection. We, as Christian parents, need to understand that our responsibility is to protect our children and deliver them from demon oppression. If you ask people how they related to their parents as children, usually people blame their parents for issues they are facing today. My father was an alcoholic, and he was often not there for his children. People can tell you about other problems and conditions they experienced in the homes they grew up in. Maybe there was insecurity or poverty because the father or mother was unable to provide for them, possibly because of addictions. Children become embarrassed and are ashamed when they grow up in homes like that. Doors are open for demons to enter during a person's childhood.

Honoring Susan

Our sons were taught to respect and honor Susan at all times and show these feelings on Mother's Day and on her birthdays definitely. Love is action.

Every year for Mother's Day, we would go into the kitchen early before church on Sunday and make breakfast. The children would help break eggs, lay sausage and bacon in skillets, put biscuits in the oven, and pour grits into boiling with butter. We would make Susan a beautiful plate of food (I like pretty food). We would wrap it nicely in foil and drive it quickly to her house. We would also take food to my mother. The boys would run in quickly because we had church to attend that morning. They were taught to give hugs and kisses, say Happy Mother's Day, and go. Later, their big sister had a baby, and we did the same thing for her. We did not fix a Mother's Day plate for my mother-in-law because she didn't celebrate any holidays.

For Susan's birthday, I made sure she had a gift. We would talk about a present for her for weeks before her birthday. The boys were so happy to take her gifts. I remember one year they asked me if they could get her an outfit. I said sure. We went shopping and picked out a two-piece outfit. We wrapped it and took it to her. Later, when the boys started working, I made sure they used their own money to purchase gifts for Susan.

Custody of Our Fourth Son

Susan was in jail for selling drugs, and Rodney was at home with no guardian. Even though his biological father is my cousin, we loved him as much as we loved my husband's sons. We wanted the best for him too, as we did for the other three boys. He was our third son's best friend, so it was a good thing to put them back together again. Rodney always cried to come over to our house before we got custody of him. He would cry, "I want to go to Daddy's house too." I would cry, too, trying hard not to let it be known. Susan would say, "Abraham is not your daddy. You can't go."

I started to ask over and over if Rodney could come too. Sometimes she would let him and other times she said no. It hurt me to leave him and take his three brothers. I prayed to God about it; after a few years or so, we did get custody of him too.

Our Sons Lived a Great Life

We took many trips and summer vacations with our kids. Candy Cane Beach, Malasses Corn Beach, Water Park, Disney World, Washington DC, Largest Water Park, King mile Lake and New Orleans. The kids enjoyed local riverboat rides, especially when we could eat prime rib dinners. They also enjoyed shopping, especially at Toys "R" Us, and especially when it wasn't for any special day and we were just enjoying life, purchasing electric cars and other things they wanted. The boys loved to shop at Toys "R" Us because it was so much to choose from such a large collection of toys.

They all had birthday parties, sometimes at home, sometimes at parks, and sometimes at Kiddie Wheel Town. We also had parties at our Family life Center at New Direction Church, at restaurants, and at arcades and tree houses.

Riverboat Tickets

We were favored when a friend gave us free tickets to ride on a riverboat. A gentleman who was also on the boat was so angry; he said, "Why are these kids on this river boat eating prime rib? My kids are at home eating hot dogs!" We just smiled and didn't say a word. He didn't like it at all. Some people just hate to see anybody enjoying life. Our sons lived a great life; they were celebrated not tolerated!

Holidays

The boys sometimes stayed inside and helped me in the kitchen peeling potatoes, washing meat, cracking eggs, and chopping celery and onions. I was always teaching them something while we worked in the kitchen—life skills with regard to Satan's tricks on adults, money issues, women, and how they should never hit girls. We laughed and had lots of fun in the kitchen.

We watched a lot of movies together. They loved to watch the same movies over and over again. I also made sure they were helping their dad with the cars in the backyard. The Bible says train up a child, so the boys did a hold lot of washing and folding clothes, cleaning bedrooms and bathrooms, vacuuming the carpets, and cleaning closets out. The chores they did as children made them feel helpful and responsible as young adults. They always did love baking cookies with me, ever since they were four and five years old. There was usually no special occasion; we just did it for fun. They did house chores all the time, but during holidays we would clean more effectively and thoroughly. Lots of family members came by to get plates of food or just visit us, enjoying the holidays together.

Walt Disney World, Florida, Youth Church Trip with New Direction Church

We spent months selling Krispy Kreme Doughnuts two or three times a month; we made the time to do this. My husband and I, on the weekends, would sit in front of grocery stores or whatever store allowed us to stand or sit. We taught the boys by example how to ask a person to buy a box of doughnuts. They sometimes didn't like delivering the sales presentation, but they finally got good at it. Yes, they sold enough to go on the trip, and for the hotel. For four sons we required a lot of money; we sold a lot of doughnuts. They put the work in. We helped them, of course, and when they got tired, they would take a break. We sold so many boxes! When I would see people on the days when we were not selling doughnuts, they would say, "Hello, Mrs. Doughnut Lady."

Fishing

On a many occasions, Abraham took our sons fishing at a private pond. When they got back, they would be so excited about the fish they had caught, and they would tell me all about their fishing expedition.

Paint Ball

This game was played with all the men and their sons from our church, New Direction. They all loved this game. They had to wear a lot of clothes so they wouldn't feel the sting of the paint ball.

Skating and Bike Riding

The boys' father is known as The Skate Master. Abraham is an excellent skater, the best I have ever seen. He loved taking all his sons to the skating rink; now he takes the grandchildren skating. I skate, too, but my skills are nothing like his. I was always trying to get better—as good as he is—but, of course, that never will happen. On some of our family bike rides, we would ride nine to ten miles all over the city.

Boy Scouts

Abraham and all the boys went to the Boy Scout meeting once a month, which was held at a church or at the leader's house. They made cars and painted them. They didn't win the racing competition, but they looked good. We still have them in a small box. The Boy Scouts also enjoyed building campfires and roasting marshmallows and hot dogs. When they went on hiking trips, they did bird watching and leaf collecting.

Pee Wee Football

We did a lot of traveling with the football teams. They won some games, and they lost some games. They all played well. They played Pop Warner. Their outfits were red and white. I can still hear their excitement about the new uniforms imprinted with their last names. All those games kept us busy, but it was awesome and exciting, screaming for them to run and watching them do their best. They loved to play football. It taught them discipline and how to play as part of a team.

Abraham Built a Tree House in our Backyard

Our sons loved to spend time in their tree house, playing and reading. That was their hangout. They invited many of their friends over to play in it with them. They had wiener roasts, parties in the backyard, and they enjoyed their tree house and birthday parties. I enjoyed making different kinds of foods for their parties.

The Rhodes Ferry Park

On Sundays after church, Abraham and I loved to go to the park with the boys. This park was across the street from our home. Abraham would play football with the boys. Keeping my weight down has always been on my mind, so whenever we went to the park, walking was my thing. It was a weekly routine to go over to the park so the boys could swing, climb on the monkey bars, run, scream, and generally have fun.

When it rained, they would skate in the large room that was our upstairs area. It may not look so large now, but back then they were young boys and small.

Sometimes on Sundays we would ride to Birmingham and have a picnic in a nice park. I would pack three or four blankets along with books to read. We'd stop and pick up fruit, cheese, meats, juices, chips, deserts and other treats. We made sure we stopped at our home church and paid our tithes first before leaving home. Tithes are a protection shield. When you sow seeds, you can expect blessings from the Lord and protection from foolishness, which do exist, but not near your tent. For more information about tithes, read blessing of the tithes in Malachi Chapter 3.

The Zandee Bell Park

I loved that park. We all would go there sometimes. It's a large park, and I loved the tennis court. We purchased tennis rackets and balls so we could all play at the same time. The court was so large we would stay out there for two hours sometimes, enjoying the park and our times together. We chased after the balls more than we played!

Hear the Prophetic Word

As the years went by, our sons became teenagers. Susan began to influence the boys more and more with her lifestyle; however, three of them followed her to another state. One at a time, they moved with her. Two of them were shot, and one became homeless. The last one who went to live with her asked me to purchase him a suitcase to pack his clothes in. I had been praying about it. I prayed. I cried. It was not in my spirt that the move was a good idea for him. I said, "Son, I know in my spirit. you should go to another state and live. Stay here in Alabama." He said, "Momma, I know what I'm doing. I'm not a little boy anymore." I said, "I beg you. Please don't go. It's not going to be good for you to do this." He kept saying, "I'm not a child or your little boy." I finally said, "Okay. I told you my spirit is disturbed about this decision you're making." I hugged him with tears rolling down my face. I left him and sat in the car and cried some more. Six months went by. I received a phone call and was told that he had been shot along with another son. I prayed, "Lord, keep them alive." Yes, God did. They all are alive today and doing well.

Hear the Prophetic Word

"A wise man will hear, and will increase learning" (Proverbs 1:5 KJV).

I am not here saying that I am a know-it-all or a perfect being—not at all. But I am in Christ now, and the Blood has made me righteous. God stirs up gifts; the prophetic word is real. Matthew 10:41: "He that receives a prophet receives a prophet reward."

What I am saying is that I am walking close to God, and I have been for some time now. When I pray for you, and when I continue to lift you up about things going on in your life, whether I know or if I don't know, my spirit cannot rest when I began to cry out about a person or a situation to God. I may even advise you to follow your heart, meaning if you want listen, have an ear to hear what God speaks to you, through me. I will tell you to follow your heart. Some people have decided in their hearts to do whatever they want to do even if it hurts them. I will leave you to follow your own folly if that's what you want to do. Some people have to learn the hard way. A bought lesson is a taught lesson and gives you a T-shirt so you can remember that bad experience, all because you refused to listen and obey God, or the Chosen Vessel.

Another son of ours who moved away to be with Susan in another state was constantly on my mind. I said, "Lord, how is he doing? Lord, what's going on? I am bothered in my sleep at night." I would wake up because I couldn't sleep. I knew something was happening. I kept saying, "Lord, show me what is wrong. What is going on?" They would never call me and say how they were doing. So the Lord just kept giving me dreams showing me as I asked him to show me. God gave me a dream about the son I kept thinking about, and bothered in my sleep. He was sleeping in a car. Sometimes I could see him in a park at night. I saw him in a car in the daylight waking up and saw him in a car at night sleeping. I said, "Oh, my God! He is living in a car in a park!" I cried so hard. He would not call and tell me. I prayed, "Lord, be his protection. Watch over him for me day and night. I plead the blood of Jesus over him." I prayed at three o'clock in the morning, speaking in tongues, doing spiritual warfare. Yes, God took care of him. He lived through it and is doing well today. He told me years later he had been homeless. I said, "I knew. God showed me."

CHAPTER 8

Encouraging the Ex, Susan

On many Mondays, my off days, I would pick Susan up and take her to my salon. I would shampoo, cut, and style her hair and shape her eye brows free of charge. I would tell her that I was not her enemy, the devil was her enemy. I was not jealous. God had given me a gift; I could make women beautiful. She looked so pretty when I finished! Although Susan is a very nice-looking lady, she looked remarkable after her salon service.

I ministered to Susan many times about how much God loves her, and I loved her, and I just wanted what was best for the children. I really didn't want the mission. I told her, "Girl, please get things together in your home. I am too busy with my salon and my life. Three children is too much for me because I am really overwhelmed with ten to fifteen clients some days." As time passed, things became worse at Susan's house. It seemed as if she was just unappreciative. I do believe she said, "Oh, no. You're gonna get these children. You and Abraham are not gonna enjoy living, driving Corvettes, and traveling the world, while I raise five kids." I did share my desires with her. I just couldn't believe that my life would be spent with three little boys, and then one more plus a girl, who sometimes stayed with us. It was a lot of work, but I knew they would be blessed because obedience is better than sacrifice. God never demands anything that He does not provide for. Whatever God commands us to do He equips us to do.

55

Then later, in the mid 1990s, Susan had another child—her sixth one. Years later, in 2015 and 2016 I did her hair at home. I really demonstrated to her the love of God.

Some days I would keep the sixth child. He was so adorable, it was hard to leave him. I loved them all. Some days in our circle prayer, he would say, "Momma Sarah, can we pray for our momma?" I'd say, "Yes, baby." We all would lift her up in prayer with tears flowing. I embraced those children with my whole heart. I said, "Lord help me to love like you love."

It settled in my mind that my life was God's will for me, and there was nothing I could do about it. Today I still work with children ages five through ten in our children's church. When I was very young, I was shown so much love by many family members. I just can't understand why some parents cannot give their all and lots of love and support to their children. That's essential for a great foundation.

Although I hated my teenage life because pain and opposition were all around, I was comforted when I thought back of the joys and the love I had been given as a child, and that still helps me today. I find myself enjoying life with the kids in our children's church. They make me smile, just like I did when I was their age, and I do all I can to make sure they smile.

She Vindictively Sacrificed the Children when She Was Angry with Abraham and Me

Susan would tell babysitters and friends not to let Abraham get the children when she was mad because the child support check hadn't been sent on the day she wanted it paid. Abraham had the whole month to get it paid. We went to the courthouse and asked about the date; we were told it was due just any time before the month was out. The problem was that she never would work even after the boys were not toddlers and they all were in elementary school. There is no excuse to not be working when you have five children.

On one October day, I took some items to Susan's house for the kids, and she was so vindictive that she packed up all the items and left them on my mom's porch. She said I was buying things she couldn't afford to buy for her own kids. Of course, you know what my mom said: "You fool!" (And she added some other unfavorable and choice words.)

One year in December, because Abraham wouldn't pay her light bill, she refused to let us get the children for Christmas. We had purchased toys, clothes, games, and other presents, and had paid the child support. She was so angry she wouldn't let them come over to visit until spring. It was the week of school break. We kept the boys that whole week. Of course you know why she allowed us to have them at that time—she didn't want to be bothered all day every day for a whole week. Abraham and I had to work, so I took them to the salon with me. I would keep them at the salon until I finished work, and then we would go out to eat and go shopping for items they liked. On most Saturdays, Abraham would be off the road, so they would be with him.

One summer day on a Friday, I called Susan and asked if we could have the children for the weekend. She said yes, it would be okay. I went to her house. I knocked and I knocked, but she did not come to the door. After I stood there on the porch wondering what could have happened, Susan peeped out of the window and looked at me with hatred in her eyes. She never opened the door. (Which didn't make any sense because I had pick up the boys many times before and it was never a problem). Later the same day, the police showed up at the salon to arrest me for going over to Susan's house. I was so embarrassed. She had sworn out a warrant for harassment. Susan told a lie and said I had stood in her yard and cursed her out. I couldn't believe it. The police picked me up. I was finger printed at the jail and then taken back to the salon so I could finish working.

Later we went to court. The judge asked me if I had cursed her out. I said, "No. I did not curse her out." He asked, "Did you go over to her house?" I said, "Yes." He said, "I find you guilty because you were there." I had to pay a fine. I hadn't done anything wrong. Still I refused to quit the mission.

If You Listen to Your Children, They Will Share Their Hurts

One weekend the boys told us some mind-blowing news about an incident that happened at Susan's house. Listen to your children. They will tell everything that is going on with them. When our son Conally was in the second or third grade, Susan caught him trying to smoke a cigarette. Let me make this clear: he was in the second or third grade! Susan punished him by making him smoke the whole thing! This punishment was nonsensical and unacceptable.

The intolerable situation was building up day after day, even though God had been telling me to get the children and be a mother to them. I just wanted to see for myself if that was the right thing to do. I tried and I tested the situation. I really didn't want to believe that God was right. I know God doesn't make mistakes. I kept saying, "Really, God? Surely it's not that bad." Of course God is always right. Oh, how the eyes can fool you. That's why God said, "We walk by faith and not by sight" (2 Corinthians 5:7 NIV). My faith wasn't too strong at all at first.

You can call me disobedient. I just couldn't fathom that God wanted me to take on such a huge responsibility, especially with my husband on the road and only at home on weekends. God saw something in me that I couldn't see. In my mind, I felt as if I just couldn't do everything required and also manage the salon all day—both first and second shifts and part of a third on weekends. Of course Abraham was home on the weekends. He came home on Friday evenings, but sometimes it would be Saturday evening before he arrived home. I had to have a menu plan for each day—either eat at a restaurant or eat a home-cooked meal. I had to prepare clothes for school each day and for church on Sundays. I'm still trying to figure out how we made it. My husband hated cooking as well as preparing clothes and ironing clothes. My husband's main concern was making sure all the bills were paid and every financial need was met.

Voodoo Doctor Story

Susan and one of my regular salon clients went together to visit a voodoo doctor. Of course, my client came back and told me everything the voodoo doctor had said. Later on, Susan herself confirmed what happen during their visit with the voodoo doctor.

My client said that, as soon as they walked in, Susan began to tell the voodoo doctor what had happened. The client said the voodoo doctor said,

"I see a mother. She is so mad, she is hot, because someone has whipped her son." Susan said, "He is not her *!%!?#!* son—he is *my* son! *I'm* the mother!" The voodoo doctor said, "I'm just telling you what I see." Susan said, "My ex and his wife have sworn out a warrant, and we are going to court. I need to know—will my boyfriend go to jail or just have to pay a fine?"

The voodoo doctor said, "No, he's not going to jail. He just needs to get his money together. He will have to pay a large fine." (And, yes, he did pay.)

The voodoo doctor told Susan I was a disciple of the Lord. This happened a year before I had answered my calling to preach the Gospel for the Lord.

Susan had gone to visit the voodoo doctor because of a situation that occurred with one of our sons. Susan's boyfriend whipped our youngest son and put long marks on his thighs. We were at the Veal Meat and Veggiehouse, a restaurant in Nashville, after church. I said, "Let me go and see why it's taking him so long to come out of the bathroom."

I went to check on him. I called his name, and I said, "What's wrong? It sure is taking you a long time to come out." He said, "My legs are hurting." I said, "Open this door!" I looked at his legs. Both had long whelp marks. I said, "Who did this?" And he told me a name; it was Susan's boyfriend. I was so angry I lost my appetite. We left that restaurant. We went home and called the Department of Human Services, took pictures, and called the police. I said, "He is gonna pay for this!" This boy was only four years old. We went to the police department on Monday morning and pressed charges. The boys weren't living with us at the time; they were just visiting for the weekend.

I called Susan and said, "Whoever did this will pay for it! I have called DHS, and I have made a police report." Susan begged me to leave it alone and just forget about it. She said the boy had pee-peed on her new sofa. I said, "That's probably because you gave him a whole soda!" I had seen her do that while I was at their house. I said, "I will not let this case go."

Car Windshield

One Sunday morning, we all were getting ready for church. When we went to get into the car, we saw that the windshield had been caved in with a very large rock. It was so big it must have taken two people to throw it in. I couldn't believe it. I cried. I was in such pain. We went to court about it, but because I didn't have any witnesses at the time, nothing could be done about it. Two of Susan's friends did share some information about what they knew, but I just left it alone and put it in God's hand. Galatians 6:7 tells us, "Be not deceived, God is not mocked, for whatsoever a man soweth, that shall he also reap" (KJV).

My mother said, "I raised you better than that. You act like I didn't have you." I said, "Momma, God has called me to preach. I'm doing all I can to please him. I will follow His will, not your will. I cannot allow you and my flesh to win. Not this time, Mom."

February 2019

Susan was locked up for unpaid child support that she owed to us. Some of her children had made several calls trying to get her out, but nothing happened. They all were so upset about it. The Spirit of the Lord touched my heart and said, "Go to Department of Human Services and have her released." So I did. I said, "Hello. I'm Sarah Haley I have come to talk to someone about a release." They thought I was wanting a man to be released. They asked me for his name. I said, "It's a lady—my husband's ex." I was sent to a back room. Another lady came out, and we sat at a table and talked. She listened to me very carefully and looked on her laptop for Susan's records. She found that Susan had never paid anything, and the case was really outdated.

"This is an old case," I said. "Please release Susan. We are good. We don't need her money anymore. Please just throw out the case." The woman agreed. The Department of Human Services sent an attorney to sign her release papers the same day, and Susan was released. Her case was thrown out the system for good. Praise God! She is released from the debt.

Susan's daughter and others had repeatedly called DHS and the jail, but nothing had happened. I give the Glory to God. I walk with God daily and have a relationship with Him. Yes, so shall thy find favor and good understanding in the sight of God and man (Proverbs 3:4). (KJV)

Some days I would minister to Susan for one to two hours or more telling her what the Word says over and over again. Days later, we would end up in another dispute about something. She didn't want to hear encouragement from the Bible; she just wanted things to go her way, right or wrong.

Encouraging Susan

As I mentioned, some days I would pick Susan up on a Monday and cut and style her hair and shape her eyebrows. I helped her get a job at the Dollar Store that was located in the same shopping center as my salon. The manager was a client, so I talked with her and asked her to give Susan a job. Some days when I wanted to get back at her, the Lord's voice would say, "Vengeance is mine ... says the Lord" (Hebrews 10:30 NKJV). I would just cry as if I was helpless, and couldn't help myself. The old Sarah would have fought with fist, gun, bat, or stick—whatever I could get my hands on. God really did do His work in me; He changed me.

The Traps That Fell

Susan was setting traps unknowingly, but I knew very well. She thought she was going to keep the boys until they became eleven or twelve and were out of control. Then she could say, "Abraham, come and get your sons." God was showing me in advance what her intensions were.

Susan set traps of rebellion. She provided no order, no discipline, no accountability, and no moral principles. She cultivated disrespect. There was no way those children would learn the difference between right and wrong.

God was giving me flashes of different visions of what their lives would be like. Without the proper discipline, I saw one in jail for house break-ins. I saw those flashes in my head. I said, "Oh, God!' Please help me with this mission you've given me. I've got to do it!"

Some weekends Susan wouldn't let Abraham have the kids, especially if she was mad about something. On the following Monday morning, I made sure our lawyer knew about it. Our lawyer told us that, if Abraham paid his child support, he was supposed to have visitations. He printed us up an affidavit and sent it to the judge to sign. The next weekend, the police served it to Susan and demand that she meet Abraham at the courthouse with the kids. This happened one time. She never tried that again.

Notary Public

Some months when Susan felt she just was not going to do the right things for the children with child support money, she would say, "Can you and Abraham use the children's child support money and purchase their clothes for school instead of sending me the money?" Oftentimes it was winter clothes. I would say, "Okay."

I knew a man at our church who was a notary public. Abraham and I would write a letter stating that the money we had spent on the clothes was equal to the child support payment that was owed for the month, and we had bought the clothes at Susan's request. I told her, "You cannot pick up the clothes until you sign your name on the letter, and the receipt will be stapled onto the letter along with the stamp from the notary. All our names will have to be signed—my husband's, mine, yours, and the notary's." We did this time and time again. It was legal in the courts as long as all the parties were in agreement and a certified notary public stamp was on the letter and the letter was written in the month she was excepting her child support. It would stand up in court. Receipts alone were not official; we needed all the proper paperwork.

I had gone to a high-end store to pick out the nicest winter clothes for all five of the children, not just for my husband's three sons. Susan signed the letter, picked up the clothes, and sold them to her neighbor. I cried so hard when I heard what she had done. I could not believe she did that! I was flabbergasted.

I was so curious about why Susan sold the clothes that the children needed, I shared the story with a hair stylist who worked with me. I said,

"Girl. I really would like to know why!" She was from Indiana, and she said, "No one here really knows me, so I will go and ask her." I said, "You will?" She said, "Yes, I'm good at this. I will go and make a conversation with her, and I will find out why she did that. It makes no sense. It's winter, and the kids need their clothes." I gave her the address. She already knew what Susan looked like; she had met her at my salon. The stylist did go an hour later. When she came back to the salon, I said, "Did you talk to her?" She said, "Yes. She told me she just wanted to hurt you because she hates you." I cried again and again.

The Children Missed School and Missed the Bus Many Times on Rainy Days

I do believe God. I know he never lies. He just can't lie. I didn't want to believe it was necessary. I wanted to see for myself. I know God sees everything. I kept saying, "No, God, it can't be that bad." Susan kept calling me asking me to take the boys to school, over and over again.

As soon as it rained, they missed school. I said to myself. *This is nonsense.* Abraham was on the road driving his eighteen-wheeler. People who are go getters just go in the rain. We get up knowing what we need to do. We go, and weather conditions don't stop us. Susan thought she was using me—she'd get the money and I'd keep the kids and do all the work.

We, as human beings, always want to know how and why. Because, if I had five children, I wouldn't want anyone to take them from me. I had compassion for Susan; I did all I could to keep our sons with her, trying to rationalize the situation in my own mind. I didn't want all the responsibility of taking care of three boys.

Susan behaved badly in so many situations. She couldn't get the children to school. She couldn't make the PTA meetings or school plays. She couldn't get items the boys needed. She needed a ride to the bank to cash the child support check. She needed the light bill paid.

It was always something. Day after day, week after week, month after month—until we took the boys out of her house. I would show up and help; but I realized it was not going to stop the drama and her calling. Our sons would come over and say, "Momma Sarah, they calling you a fool."

I said, "What?" Our son said, "Susan and her boyfriend were laughing saying, 'Call your fool!'"

I looked and I listened the first two years, just taking notes. I said, "God, I'm sorry for not believing you. I'm trying to get pregnant with a child of my own. Here's this lady, Susan, who has all these beautiful children and she's bothering me constantly to help her with them, and you are saying get them out of her house?" God said, "I'm giving you her children." That just seems unbelievable. It really did hurt me to my core. It was not my will, but God's. I had to obey him, no matter how hard or big the load was.

The way people treat you is a statement of who they are as human beings. It's not a statement about you. Remember that.

Before we got custody of the sons, Susan asked us if we would keep the kids for one year so she could go back to school to get a GED and move out of the house that she complained about all the time.

She was always saying the light bill in this Department of Housing and Urban Development (HUD) house was too much, and the bill was getting higher and higher. Every other month it was, "Can y'all pay my light bill?" We talked a lot about a better life for Susan. I said, "What will it take for things to get better for your life? I want to see you happy, see you smile, and have true joy with your children—all of them." She said, "I can change my life if you all just keep the boys for a year." I was in agreement, so I shared with my husband all that I had discussed with Susan. He was in agreement also. The Scripture says, "How can two walk together except they agree" (Amos 3:3 KJV).

Although I knew I had orders from God to be a mother to the children, I really was afraid of the challenge of having three young boys with me at all times, except for when they were in school. I really didn't want all that responsibility. Although I loved God and loved the children, the responsibility of caring for them was a scary thought. I said, "Lord, that's a lot of children and a lot of work. Lord, I prayed for a loving, saved man, not all of this. I prayed for a man that didn't smoke or drink alcohol, a man that wasn't whorish, and definitely no ugly man, no couch potato, a working man who loves God." God did grant me my request, along with five children and said, "Be good to all of them." And I was.

She Didn't Know, and I Didn't Understand It (at First)

Susan did not realize that I was God sent; neither did I at first. I had been God sent to help her with the children and to be a voice and a mediator between her and Abraham. She wanted her way—continuous cursing and being loud. Abraham wanted his way—quiet and moody as he was angered daily by her drama. We weren't getting anywhere at all.

Abraham had *no* tolerance when it came to drama. I, on the other hand, was used to it. Even today I still feel like a private agent sent to the rescue by God in the situation to make a difference in everyone's lives in this story.

Abraham and I were married in 1990. I met him when I was twenty-five. I am fifty-five years old now. When we started this journey, it was heated for about six to seven years. Especially in 1992, the drama was over the top—*extreme!* I thank God for the mission because we made it. I also thank the Lord it's finished, as Enoch did in the Bible, I pleased God (Hebrews 11:5).

Finally I had to put on my high-heel shoes and stomp the devil under my feet in spiritual warfare. Spiritual warfare is the Christian concept of fighting against the work of preternatural evil forces. I had to get myself infused with power. Evil spirits are demons sent to intervene in human affairs in various ways. I read a book by John Eckhardt called *Prayers That Rout Demons: Prayers for Defeating Demons and Overthrowing the Powers of Darkness.* This book is a blessing. It helped me so much. I would speak the prayers out loud every day.

CHAPTER 9

———◆———

Clients Talking in the Salon

One of my clients said, "You could have three thick gold chains if you were not supporting all these kids." Another client said, "Shop at the dollar store for those kids. Don't you buy them nice things; they won't appreciate it. Do a little something to say you did something for them."

I said, "I'm not doing this so they will appreciate it. Really, it's because God told me to help them, so I'm obeying Him. I'm not worrying about any money because I know God will provide for me for helping them."

Some of the clients would say things like, "You are a business owner, doing very well. Why are you dealing with Susan and all her drama?" I told them, "I'm ordered by God to help save her children. He put me in this situation. It is the plan for my life.

My Clients Turned Against Me

"What is wrong with our hair stylist?" they all said. "Kids of another lady?" One said. "You doing too much. Stop trying to live like people on a soap opera."

I said, "I was a woman called to preach." (Someone said, "Is she crazy?") I said, "Satan hates women because it was a woman who gave birth to Jesus, and it is Jesus who has defeated Satan."

A client shot me a bird. I was mocked so badly. The things so many people said hurt me deeply.

"Girl, you want some more kids to take care of?" one client said, laughing. "Take mine. I wish I had this kind of help with my kids."

"There ain't no *!%!?#!* good enough to take care of my kids!

I said, "Girl, I know that's right." I just laughed right with them.

"So you are the one taking Susan's kids? Why are you trying to show her love? She's treating you bad. Girl, you are trying to live a soap opera life. You can't be nice to her, fixing her hair, taking her to the bank. Are you crazy or a fool?"

One of my every-two-weeks clients said, "Girl, catch me up. What has Susan done lately or last since I was here the last time?"

One thing I learned: if you try to keep all the people happy all the time, you will never fulfill your destiny.

Life Early in the Morning Tuesday through Friday and sometimes on Saturday at the House Before I Go to the Salon

I prayed to God to do something to help me get up. I was sometimes late getting the boys up for school. One morning, God sent an angel to ring the doorbell. The chimes were ringing! It was a miracle. No one was ever at the door, but the sound was there. Only God can make that happen I asked the boys if they had heard the sound, and they said no. I said, "Wow, God loves me and hears my prayers. God gave me more strength, God gave me help."

I would be so tired from doing hair all day and part of the evening. It was hard to get up and moving in the morning with three boys (at the time). But we were determined to save the boys from the traps of enemy. The teachers and the principal were asking why the boys were late. They were threatening to take me to court for too many tardies. I never went to court (thank God!). Some mornings I wanted to sit down and eat breakfast with them. The Holiday Inn buffet breakfast was perfect. It was very close to our house at 914 Stright Street. The boys told on me to the teachers one time when we were late. They told their teachers we were late because we were eating breakfast at the Holiday Inn.

Life at the Salon

The kids stayed outside playing until seven or seven thirty in the evening when I made them come in and take a nap on a pallet until I was finished working at around nine. Then I would clean a little, getting ready for the next day. I'd call the police, who would sit in the parking lot while I loaded the Crock-Pots into the trunk of the car and got the boys in their seats. Then they'd escort us all the way home.

The boys' big sister lived with us for about two or three months. She would wash my shop towels, with the boys help. I would start the machine, and all they had to do was take the towels from the machine, put them in dryer, fold them up, and bring them back to the shop. I paid her for helping out especially during the summer because she wanted to buy her mother gifts. God blessed my hands to make a lot of money.

My clients gave the children money for snacks. There was a Center City Grocery in the shopping center, and I gave them money for snacks too. They didn't want for anything.

Life Before and After I Took the Children to School and Returned to the Salon for Work

Some mornings, I would give the boys milk and cereal. Some mornings, I would give them breakfast bars and cartons of milk in the car on the way to the school. They had to read a scripture before they get out the car. I would talk about it and explain it. The main one was <u>"A little slumber a little folding of the hands and poverty will creep up on you like a bandit"</u> <u>(Proverbs 24:33–34 KJV)</u>.

Finally, I would head to the salon with my two Crock-Pots, meat, and vegetables. I would stop and pick up a dozen hush puppies, which was down the street from the salon. This would be their bread. At 2:45 I would leave the clients under the dryer and walk to the back of the school to meet the boys at the bus stop at the elementary school on Hero's Drive. They would eat first and do their homework second. Only then would they watch television or go outside on their skateboards. Some days, I would batter potato wedges and drop them into a FryDaddy to sell to my customers or customers at the barber shop behind my salon. By doing this, I was teaching the children that you can make money just by putting forth an effort, and they loved that.

My salon was called Sarah's Magic Shears. Susan told the kids it was called Sarah's Magic Bologna. Before we received custody, the boys would come over to visit, and they kept saying Sarah's Magic Bologna. I said, "What? Who said that?" They were small, and the oldest one said, "Our momma said it. She said your shop is called Sarah's Magic Bologna."

A Prophetess Came by the Salon with a Word for Abraham, Me, and Our Sons

The prophetess told me first that I was called to preach, which I already knew at the time, although I hadn't mentioned it to anyone because I was so afraid and felt I was too unqualified to do something like that. She said I was not hot or cold but lukewarm, and if I didn't change my ways, God said He would spew me out of his mouth. She spoke some awesome things about Abraham, but I can't mention them.

She looked at our three sons and said, "That one right there, the devil has a trap set for him to take him down. "I said oh no." It was in 1995. I just couldn't see that. Twenty-four years later it most definitely almost happen, but with much praying and standing on the Word, we saw God deliver him out of that trap the enemy had set.

After Leaving the Salon One Weekend

Sometimes, we would go to a restaurant. The children would take turns choosing a restaurant according to what he felt like eating—hamburgers, pizza, Mexican food, Chinese food. After we ate, if it was summer and they were out of school, we would drive for twenty to twenty-five minutes to Krispy Creme Doughnuts in another city, and get fresh doughnuts if the light was on. Oh my, hot and fresh out the fryer! We'd get home at midnight or one in the morning. They loved pizza restaurants more than all the other restaurants.

Some days I would start doing hair and couldn't stop. I wouldn't have time to get the Crock-Pots started, but at 2:45, I would leave to get them from school. The clients would be under the dryers or just waiting for me to get back. I had to go. A barbeque restaurant was across the street from the salon. Sometimes, I had to go over and get chicken sandwiches and Brunswick stew with potatoes—very good—and crackers for supper. God always made a way for us.

CHAPTER 10

The Word of God Works

"Mix the Word with faith" (Hebrews 4:2 KJV).

Know this: the fight was already won before it began.

"The fight is never about man or to hurt man, but it's about that evil spirit that exalts itself against the knowledge of our God" (2 Corinthians 10:5 KJV).

So God shows us through his word and real situations that He is a supernatural God, and victory belongs to Him and His followers. He shows us what looks impossible to man is possible with Him (Luke 18:27).

My pastor, Dr. D. Jackson, said, The Word of God works when you work the Word. If it's not working for you, it's because you're not working it and not believing it. Speak it, decree it, declare the Word over every situation and over all challenges you encounter. "If only I knew these scriptures in the beginning of my mission."

Speak the Word out of your mouth as many times as you need to so you can believe it's working in you through faith; only then will you soon see it manifest before your eyes. Hebrews 4:2 tells us that the word won't profit you if you don't mix it with faith.

Time for Spiritual Warfare—No Pretty Prayers

One of our sons said he was going to commit suicide. He had to learn to fight in the Spirit. He called me on my cell phone at around 11:30 one night, and we talked until midnight. Then I felt in my heart I needed to go and pick him up. I said, "Where are you?" He said, "At my girlfriend's and her father's house." After we talked a while, he was crying, and he said, "Momma, thank you for all you have done for me. I'm out of here. I'm killing myself. I'm out of here. I can't live no more. I just wanna say I really do appreciate all you have done for me." I was crying. I said, "son, what's wrong? Why do you feel you need to do something like this?" I just kept crying, listening to him. Finally I thought to myself, *It doesn't matter what time it is or the reason—there's no reason ever to do this. I'm going to get this son.*

I grabbed my keys and left home. I went to the girlfriend's house inflamed. I was mad at the enemy—38 hot! The Durango's lights flashed on the house. I left them on and the motor running. I jumped out. I knocked on the door, he came out and got in the truck with me. I said, "We are going to the church. When we got there, I turned the lights on. I said, "The devil is a liar—the father of lies! You will not kill yourself tonight and no other night, young man!" I started giving him affirmations, one after another and speaking to the demonic forces. I started binding up the Spirit of suicide. I started speaking to our son about who he was. "You are a king! You are royalty! You are shaped in God's image. You are strong in the Lord and in the power of His might. Jesus died on the cross for you, and Jesus reigns over every principality. All power is in His hand. Jesus loves you, son. You are an overcomer, a world overcomer. You will overcome this mess with your girlfriend! I plead the Blood of Jesus over your mind. Your thoughts are good thoughts, not evil." I was touching his chest and his head, telling him, "You shall live and not die!" repeatedly.

At New Direction Church, my pastor had taught me how to do spiritual warfare. I was determined to snatch our son out of Satan's hand and his traps that night. I prayed and prayed for hours. He ran around the church speaking what I was saying. Then I started running around the church too with him. He was a delivered young man Then we left the church. Praise be to God He delivered our son. We were stinky and tired and hungry, we went to the Waffle House and he was free indeed. We had great laughter and joy while eating together. You must choose the Word to defeat the enemy. It works! I'm a witness that it does.

A Word of Encouragement to Fathers: You Will Win

Fathers, please do not walk out of your children's lives. They need you, not later—they need you right now. Be bold and courageous. Go get your sons and daughters. I can't say it enough. Visit with them on weekends; know what's going on all during the week. Make it your business. It's crucial. If you don't, who will?

Make sure the environment of your children is comfortable, beneficial, and suitable so they can be productive citizens in life. Make sure that they are doing their homework and they can focus to do their homework. Make sure you are providing for the children. Make sure they have the things they need such as clothes, shoes, coats, school supplies, money, and whatever else they need. All these things help make up an environment conducive to positive growth. Please let them know by telling them out loud. Say "I love you." Action is important; it creates well-being. They need to hear it: "I love you, son." "I love you, daughter." "I'm here for you, even if I don't live in the same house with you."

Do all you can to support the children together with their mother and your new wife. Ecclesiastes 4:12: "A three-fold cord is not easily broken" (NLT). Psalm 133:1 NIV- Come together in unity" (NIV). Psalm 133:3 "There the Lord commanded the blessing" (NIV).

If the environment is inappropriate, over the top, and the mother is not being a good mother on a consistent level, and an abundance of foolishness is happening daily, do what it takes to get your children out of that terrible situation. Sending money or buying things sometimes is not enough. We all have heard that a child is a product of his or her environment. Be sure to make it a great one.

I'm not suggesting that all fathers need to take custody of their children, please understand. All I'm saying is do not pretend as if all is well, ignoring a situation because of fear or laziness or too many jobs when a matter can be handled now before it's too late. After sixteen or seventeen years, you will be in tears, wishing that you had paid more attention and given them more of your time long ago. We cannot go back in time and fix or change anything. After time has gone by, it's too late.

Proverbs 22:6 says, "Train up a child in the way he should go, and when he is old, he will not depart from it" (KJV). This is the parents' responsibility; it is not the responsibility of law enforcement or teachers at the school.

Yes, it's work, but it's also worth it. It's worth the sacrifice.

A Word of Encouragement to Mothers: You Will Win

Mothers, if you are single, married, or divorced and have children from the relationship, please allow the father of the children and his new wife, if he has one, to be part of the children's lives.

It was never God's plan for the mother to have all the responsibility of raising children alone. Proverbs 23:22: "Hearken unto thy father that begat thee" (KJV).

How can they listen to their father if he's never around or you won't allow him to be around? Do all you can to live in peace with the father of your children. Romans 12:18 says, "If it be possible, as much as lieth in you, live peaceably with all men" (KJV). Yes, you have to work at it. It can be difficult at first. Just be persistent, and you'll see great results soon. It really can be a wonderful life when we include the Word of God in the situation. Although God was speaking and guiding me, I wasn't mature enough to see that at the beginning of our situation. I finally realized that, if I wanted peace and a healthy relationship with Susan, the only way was through the Scriptures and trusting God in every matter. In keeping steadfast in God's Word and much prayer, we did overcome, and victory was ours. We won through Jesus Christ our Lord and Savior, and so can you.

> "Being confident of this, that he who began a good work in you will carry it on to completion until the day of Christ Jesus" (Philippians 1:6 NIV).
>
> Ecclesiastes 1:9 teaches us, "The thing that hath been, it is that which shall be; and that which is done is that which shall be done: and there is no new thing under the sun" (KJV).

This is what I meant but I couldn't explain it to people. What God was doing through me was already finished. Long before God whispered to me and said, "Be a mother to these children," I had already done it; I already had accepted the challenge. I just didn't know it at the time. It had been done in heaven already. God just allowed me to go through the process of achieving it. He knew it was going to be rough and tough for me. He knew almost everyone around me was going to be against me. Statistics have proven that 10 percent of people who know you won't like you, no matter what you do. He knew I was going to be cursing, angry, frustrated, and so disappointed about the many obstacles that were in my way. That's the reason He was speaking to me, giving me so many dreams. He showed me a movie script of the boys being in trouble. He would say, "This is what their lives are going to be like if you don't obey me and help them." Why do you think that, before you go see a movie, the preview has already been shown on TV? The reason is that it has already been recorded; it's finished.

Dr. Myles Monroe, Bahamian evangelist and minister, once said, "The greatest tragedy in life is not death, but life without purpose."

I was willing to die for our sons' lives and also my husband's. I was a helpmate to my man. I used to say every day, "Over my dead body will Susan destroy my husband and his sons!"

I was dedicated and committed to the call and the charge or mission God had put in my mind and heart and my spiritual ears. I became obsessed with it. It was my passion and my purpose from God. I knew I was pleasing God!

I grew up in church. I heard the pastor say every Sunday how many want to hear the Lord say, "Well done, my good and faithful servant.

Welcome home, you been faithful over a few things" (Matthew 25:21 NIV). I would say to myself, *I want to hear the Lord say that.* My pastor would also say that Jesus got up with all power. Every Sunday I said to myself, *I want power too.*

I got that Holy Ghost power. I win! I mean, I win by working the Word of God. The devil can't win with the Word I use. My Word is my Bible; it is my weapon, my tool. I win, people of God. So can you! Get your Bible out and start winning.

You Can Win—You Are More Than a Conquer through Christ Jesus

I do not know what you are facing; neither do I know your struggle. Dr. D. Jackson, our pastor, said, "If the Word is not working for you, you're not speaking it or believing it, but I do know this, if you want to win in God you can win with His method of operation."

Galatians 6:7–9: "Do not be deceived: God cannot be mocked. A man reaps what he sows. Whoever sows to please their flesh, from the flesh will reap destruction; whoever sows to please the Spirit, from the Spirit will reap eternal life. Let us not become weary in doing good, for at the proper time we will reap a harvest if we do not give up" (NIV).

Isaiah 55:11: "So shall my word be that goeth forth out of my mouth: it shall not return unto me void, but it shall accomplish that which I please, and it shall prosper in the thing whereto I sent it" (KJV).

Proverbs 18:12: "Death and life is in the power of your tongue, he that love it shall eat the fruit there of" (KJV).

Job 22:28: "If you decree a thing it shall be so, (so do not decree what you don't want). You just may get it" (KJV).

The Word of God works! I did this. I know it works. Put the Scriptures that relate to your problem in your mind. Write down six or seven scriptures every week, and you will get results. Keep them with you to look at as many times in a day as you can. Meditate on them.

When you praise God, He'll make his presence known because, when praises go up, blessings do come down. God inhabits the praises of His people. When you learn the Word, quote daily those verses that you need for your specific problem. Believe that Scripture. The word really does work for any person who will take the time to meditate on it. Speak it out of your mouth as often as you feel necessary—in the morning before work, in your car while driving to work, while you are on break, when you return home, and just before bed.

And don't be afraid to say, "Satan, I rebuke you! You are a liar and the father of lies. Go in the name of Jesus! I belong to God. God is my strength. God is my joy, and the joy of the Lord is my strength. Victory belongs to me. I win, you lose again, Satan. I am more than a conqueror, through Christ Jesus that strengthens me."

Even if you don't feel like it, even if you don't see results right away, keep on doing this. It will feel strange at first, but just keep doing it. It's always a strange feeling when you do something for the first time. It may feel odd speaking what you can't see that it hasn't manifested yet. Keep speaking it until you see it come to pass.

Just keep doing it, if you want to win in God. Keep doing it—daily, weekly, monthly. It's not hard. Do it instead of speaking the old words you used to say and cursing the situation. Change your words. If you complain, it means you will remain, and the problem will be magnified bigger and greater. Please speak the Word of God if you want to win. Stop being so frustrated and angry with daily headaches and moods and people all day. It's not them. It's the devil using the people to keep you feeling sad, mad, and hateful. Ephesians 6:12 says, "We wrestle not against flesh and blood" (KJV).

Pray for the Co-Parent Too

We love praying. Honestly, it was not easy to pray for my husband's ex-wife. I haven't always been able to bless Susan. There were times in our marriage when we wouldn't mention her name. We just said "she" or "the ex." By the time our sons started middle school, we were able to pray for and speak blessings on Susan.

During our seasons with Susan, there was so much drama—unnecessary drama, hurt, and pain. I cried so much. My husband is not like me, crying about all the many disappointments we had to deal with because of Susan, day after day, week after week, month after month. I believe Susan was doing all she could to drive me crazy. I realized that only prayer could keep me safe and strong. Although I prayed, it took time and years for me to not be angry with Susan. My anger became a motivating force. The anger was distracting me at first. The distraction was causing me to become discouraged. Susan wanted me to be discouraged so I would walk away, so I could flip the switch. Prayer is so powerful, so I prayed even more.

Pray for the co-parent two or three times a day, and include his or her name in your prayer list, it's necessary. Pray the best of life, health, peace, and understanding for the co-parent. Pray that God shines His face on him or her. The children love all the parents. This love gives them peace, and their faces glow when they hear you speaking blessings on the other parents. This is my story, what I experienced. I was strengthened when I started to pray for Susan. I had to stay focused, I realized finally that it was God's will for me to stay my course. When God gives you a mission, you have to stand and fight the good fight of faith.

Don't Try to Be or Play God Over Your Situation, As I Did in the Beginning

Cast that care—your burdensome situation—on God. Only then will God strengthen you through it. You'll get peace. Yes, it may look bad, but cast the burden on God. Just say, "God, it's too big for me. Take it from me. I invite you to come in and handle this." Our fight was tough and long;

it lasted for years, all because at the beginning I wasn't casting it on God. Instead I was trying to handle it on my own or in my own strength. That made it impossible. "With God all things are possible" (Matthew 19:26 NIV). Without Him you can do nothing (John 15:5). I began to see my problems as water rolling down a duck's back. I let God sustain me. Finally, peace was mine after I gave my problems to God. And it can be yours too.

Go to sleep. Don't stay up angry and worrying and plotting. Trust God. Put your life in God's hands. God never sleeps or slumbers; both of you don't need to be up all night. Pray for every person involved in the situation. When you cover everyone in prayer, it shows God that your heart is pure and you have no hidden motive. It also shows God that you love as He does. God is love. He is not the author of confusion, and He loves everyone—yes everyone. God loves us all unconditionally. The Word of God gives us peace. I didn't know that at first. I learned after Pastor Jackson started training us and teaching us the gospel in ways I had never heard it taught before. I said, "Wow, is this the same Bible?" He was teaching so that I could see myself winning. I love winning strategies. God doesn't want us living defeated.

The Enemy Has Set Traps

Do not allow the traps that the enemy has set to be your story. No one likes listening to a sad story about your children that could have been avoided. We must give the children the best foundation we can give. Fight hard to prevent them from falling into the enemy's traps. Do it in love and with the grace of God. Let's eliminate excuses.

1. I didn't know all this was happening in their lives.
2. I lived ten hours away from my children.
3. I was working two or three jobs, and I really didn't have the time. I had to pay my bills.
4. I remarried and my new partner was a stumbling block.

Here are some of the traps the enemy uses to ambush our children:

1. Drug addition

2. Peer pressure
3. Alcohol addiction
4. Stealing, lying, and other devious behavior
5. Rejecting the Bible
6. Choosing the wrong partner or mate
7. Prison
8. Low self-esteem
9. Premature death
10. Suicide

Teach your children to be prayerful and watchful with a discerning spirit.

Dr. D. Jackson says "Excuses are smoke screens for the uncommitted."

Be committed to your children; they are yours. Many people are working so hard, trying to achieve the American dream, but they are ignoring their own children. Twenty years later, they end up with an American nightmare that brings long-term heartache, shame, and embarrassment.

Be active in your children's lives. Know all the babysitters. Do background checks. Give them "that" look (you had better not think about doing anything bad to my children!). Ask all kinds of questions when you return home. Install a camera if you feel the need to, or just get the children away from harmful places and persons.

Please pray with all your children, because they will be gone soon. The time moves quickly, believe me. All your children will pray when they are older if they see you pray today. Proverbs 22:6: "Train up a child in the way he should go: and when he is old, he will not depart from it" (KJV).

Fathers and mothers, kneel down with your children while they are young. Explain to them, "This is prayer time." You can pray standing up or kneeling before God. Just pray. They won't ever forget it.

When we become an example to our children as we go on our knees, we show humility—being humble before our God. He is Lord of the earth, and everything in it belongs to Him. He is God (Jahve) of the Universe. It seems more intimate and the praying seems to be more effective when you tell the children you are expecting a change in a situation or a need to be met. Tell them, "We love God. God is our source, and we greatly revere and praise and worship Him. We depend on Him. Our hope is in Him. We bow down only to this one great God and no other. He is our King, Lord, and our Savior who has all power in heaven and earth." When the prayer is answered, remind the children about how you were kneeling down together praying for a change or the thing that God did provide for you. When I was a little girl, my aunt use to do that with me all the time. I didn't understand. I was only between the ages of two and five. Now when trouble that's bigger than me shows up, or I need something I don't have, I know to get on my knees and pray.

God had to bring it back to my remembrance.

Romans 7:18: "In me (that is, in my flesh,) dwelleth no good thing" (KJV). You can only fight wars in the flesh for so long, if you were taught to bow down, give it to God through prayer, you will go back to it. I did.

Postures of Prayer

Children are always interested to hear that there are different positions for prayer other than head bowed with eyes close. We taught our children to pray using different methods, as long as they were undistracted, they could pay attention, and they showed respect to God.

Here are some Bible passages that reference different methods of praying:

Kneeling: 2 Chronicles 6:13, Acts 9:40

Standing: 1 Kings 8:22, Mark 11:25

Lifting up hands: Psalm 28:2, 1 Kings 8:22

Bowing: Genesis 24:26, Matthew 2:11

Face down before God: Joshua 5:14, Matthew 26:39, Numbers 16:22. (In this position, our boys would pretend they were praying, but sometimes they would fall asleep. We would then stand up and pray.) (Ha ha ha, we still laugh about this today when we get together).

CHAPTER 11

Department of Human Services

The Department of Human Services told us that, if they became involved, they would separate the boys and place them in different homes that were available. They would divide them so that all five would have different addresses. Yes, we called DHS on Susan and her boyfriend and mentioned some things that had taken place in the home. They said, "If you all are concerned parents, you don't need to call us. What you need to do is get a lawyer and take the children out of that situation."

We already had asked the mother for the children. We explained to Susan that we knew about many wrong things that were happening. I begged her to change their lifestyle. She said Abraham couldn't run her house and his house too. We finally came to the conclusion that we didn't want the children to end up in the system where they would be separated. We had no choice but to get them out as soon as possible or they would be in a prison system later on. The system is not designed for us; that is not God's plan.

We became definitely concerned and serious. We needed to stop talking about it, and walk it instead because we loved our kids and wanted better lives for them. A foster home is not always the best solution. In some cases the children are placed with loving and caring families. In many cases, foster kids are mistreated; some are abused physically, sexually, verbally, emotionally, and so on. It's a risk. I do know many great foster parents that have done an excellent job. They love God, have Christian homes, and have been amazing parents to many children.

The Department of Human Services will Scatter Your Children

Open your eyes and ears and know for yourself what is happening in the home where your children live. Our sons' home with their mother was not a good environment. Many things were going on during those years and continued to go on year after year. Of course, we didn't want to believe it. It was very hard for me to accept. I kept saying, "How can this be?" Having beautiful children is a blessing from the Lord. A mother should do all she can to love and protect her children from all drugs and evil in this world. A mother should fear losing her children when she knows what she's doing can send her to jail.. We refused to allow statistics to win. I pray that you are not a drug user or seller. In our sons' case, drugs were being used and sold and cooked. You cannot use or traffic in drugs and parent children at the same time. Drug use is a form of child neglect. Parents who are involved in drugs are not able to concentrate or make sound judgments for their children.

CHAPTER 12

———◆◆◆———

My Husband and I Started a Nonprofit Organization

Abraham filed for 501(C)(3) nonprofit status. Our organization was called Winners Medallions. Our colors were purple and white.

We started Winners Medallions out of love for all children who were just like the ones we were saving from the traps of the enemy. We were so concerned about them and so compassionate about them, we wanted to see them thrive. We wanted to fill them with long-lasting memories that would make a positive impact on their lives forever. We started out going door to door, just praying with families in their homes and yards. We kept saying we need a building so we could do more. New Direction Church allowed us to use The Meeting Place. We also used their church bus to pick up families. Our Quest van was only big enough for about ten children, and we tried that at first, making two and three trips each day.

Days of operation for Winners Medallions were Monday, Tuesday, and Wednesday. We picked up the children between four and four thirty. Until six thirty, we held homework tutorials for twenty-five to thirty kids and fed them a meal. Once a month, Ryan's Buffet restaurant would feed them for free because of our nonprofit status. The children had to bring only one dollar for tips. We owe a debt of thanks to them.

We formed a basketball team and cheerleaders. We ordered uniforms for the boys from Lang's Sporting Goods. Mrs. Katie Davis made cheerleading outfits for the girls, and we thank her! Mrs. Missy White helped me prepare food some days. Mr. Chris White helped us often with boys' haircuts and classes also. We thank everyone for their help. I would do the girls hair and nail polish. My husband also taught classes and arts and crafts, and how to make a neck tie, air brush, change tires (boys only).

We took trips to parks, water parks, and go-kart tracks. We went to the Museums. We took them to movies, and we had slumber parties at our home.

Adult Classes

In 1997, we picked up adults for morning classes we called Lunch with the Word. My husband taught hope classes, and our Apostle Jackson also taught hope classes. Minister Shelly Walls taught classes also during the day. Loving volunteer cooks also helped us. Lunch was served last. We opened the floor so everyone could share their thoughts after class. We served soups, cakes, casseroles, sandwiches, and other nourishing foods. I express thanks in loving memory of Mother Jessie Sanders, Mother Reshonda Waters, Mrs. Molly Chairs, and Mother Kathy Ross. And we thank New Direction Church for all their support.

Local business made donations to help us: Center City Grocery and Walmart donated food vouchers. McCullum's Catfish, Wright Smocked Barbecue, and Samson Iron Shop donated checks. Creek Funeral Home donated cash. Mrs. Sally Wright donated food from the elementary school PTA meetings. And many more sowed seeds. Great thanks to you all!

Winners Medallions started in 1996 and ran for almost seven years. God was really working in us to help children and families. We had to do something; it was in our hearts. We kept saying that so many children just like ours needed help, love, and attention. We touched a lot of lives back then. We were going door to door praying with people asking them, "Are you saved?" We led so many to Christ. We prayed till drunk men became sober.

We kept saying to ourselves, *This is hope.* The people can have victory in their situations. We wanted to see them smile and experience the joy of the Lord. We wanted to see them *win* in this race through Christ Jesus. Our Apostle Jackson became a covering umbrella over us when we joined New Direction Church. We are forever thankful for all the help that was given to us.

Winners Medallions made floats for the Christmas parade each year. We really had a wonderful experience serving the people of God. All the children were part of the parade and our New Direction Church family. We were some radical young people for Christ.

Winners Medallions, unfortunately, could not last forever; we needed more structure and more money to keep going to higher heights for today's demands.

CHAPTER 13

———— ✦ ————

Questions to Ask Yourself

Questions for Mothers, Ex-Wives, and New Wives

1. Why are you so angry? Anger is nonsense.
2. Why do you hate your baby daddy's new wife? She makes him smile again, and now he is serving the Lord and reading God's word with his new wife.
3. Have you taken the time to get to know her?
4. Why would you allow ten or more years to pass without your child seeing his father when he wants to? That is nonsense.
5. Is it because he has a new lady friend or a new wife, you don't want him to see his children because you want him to see the children only when you both are together? Why? That is nonsense.
6. What's your motive? It's complicated, right? Is it so you can sleep together (again)? Is it so you and he can ride to the nearest side store or mall or restaurant? Is it so you can be free to talk about your past relationship, because you still have hopes of getting back together?
7. If your baby daddy has a wife, why do you think it's okay to invite him only to holiday gatherings, birthday parties, and graduations? That is nonsense. Why send one invitation instead of two when he is married now? Do you think he should show up? The two have

become one. Twenty years have passed. Why are you still angry? Why do you reject his wife? Whose fault is it?

8. How do you plan to have a family with your baby daddy who is married? The two have become one (Genesis 2:24).

9. Why lie to the children and say his new wife broke up your marriage when you are the one who broke it up, and you know you did? That is nonsense.

10. Why tell the father he can pick up his child/children, and after he has driven for miles to get them, you change your mind? That is nonsense.

11. Why you don't want the father to see the children now that he has a new baby in his new marriage? That is nonsense.

12. Why is it when the father sends gifts, you scratch the father's name out and put your name on the gifts? That is nonsense.

13. Why is it that, when the father has a child from a previous relationship, you don't want that child around. Why you don't want him to support that child? But you want him to help support the previous children you had when he met you? That is nonsense, and it is selfish.

I know we all remember the R&B singer Stephanie Mills. She recorded the song "I have Learned to Respect the Power of Love," which was written by Angela Winbush and René Moore. Don't pretend to be blind. Respect the man or woman's new love. It's over with you. Move on. God has another plan for you. Bless them; they'll respect you all the more. Try it.

Questions for Fathers, Ex-Husbands, and New Husbands

1. You are the father. Why do you refuse to support your child or children? That is nonsense.

2. Why do you say the child is not yours? The child looks just like you! That is nonsense.

3. If you are not sure, why haven't you taken a blood test? You can pay for a blood test. It's a small fee. Or you can pick up a DNA kit at any number of stores.

4. Why do you pick up your child for a funeral but never pick up the child for weekend visitations? That is nonsense.

5. Now that the children are successful and don't need your money anymore, you want to claim the child and give your long speech about why you were not there or not supportive. That is nonsense. Please don't allow that to be you.

6. Why will you help support your new wife with her child or children that she had before she met you, and you had children or child before you met her and will not help them? That is nonsense.

7. Why are you so angry that your ex-wife has a new husband and he is helping support your children? That is nonsense.

8. Why now you feel you shouldn't do anything? That is nonsense.

9. Why is it that you stop supporting your child or children after you have one or two more children in a new relationship? That is nonsense.

10. Fathers should love all the children. If you're all in the same house, it doesn't make a difference whose children live there. That is nonsense.

11. If one job is not enough, you may need two jobs. Maybe you should take up a new trade or career.

There are some great fathers who do support their children: These questions I've asked are not for them! Praise God for all of you—you are wonderful examples and number-one dads! You please God.

Marriage Covenant Scriptures for the Children, Ex-Spouses, and New Spouses

1. Problems usually start when a child or another person can separate a marriage union for birthday parties, graduations, ball games, holiday gatherings, and any other events or special occasions. "So they are no longer two but one flesh, what therefore God has joined together, let no man separate" (Matthew 19:6 NIV). Send two invitations; that's respect.

2. "Likewise, husbands, live with your wives in an understanding way, showing honor to the woman as the weaker vessel, since they are heirs with you of the grace of life, so that your prayers may not be hindered" (1 Peter 3:7 ESV).

3. "However, let each one of you love his wife as himself, and let the wife see that she respects her husband" (Ephesians 5:33 ESV).

4. "He who finds a wife finds a good thing, and obtains favor from the Lord" (Proverbs 18:22 NKJV). He'll find you; just seek God.

5. "Then the Lord God said, 'It is not good that the man should be alone; I will make him a helper fit for Him'" (Genesis 2:18 ESV).

Let God do his business, He knows who is fit for you. It's nonsense crying for a man you're not fit for.

Fathers: Take Care of Your Families

"Anyone who does not provide for his own, and especially for those of his own house, he hath denied the faith, and is worse than an unbeliever" (1 Timothy 5:8 NIV).

Covenant with God

I pray that every person reading this book is saved. I have a message for you: You may have messed up. You may be in trouble or hot water with your spouse. Repent to God! Ask your spouse for forgiveness. Jesus Christ paid the price on the cross for our sins. You can be forgiven and find yourself back in place with God. We are also the seed of Abraham; we are in covenant with God. It's our covenant that moves God's hand; that's why he keep showing up to help us. Yes, he hears your cry. Just believe! Even when you do wrong, repent and cry out to God. He hears your cry, your groaning, and your deep pain. He heard the children of Israel (Exodus 2:24). God heard their groaning, and God remembered his covenant with Abraham. Exodus 1:23 says, "And they cried, and their cry came up unto God" (KJV).

The covenant is activated on your behalf; put pressure on the covenant. God cannot lie; He will do what His word says. The children of Israel worshiped another god and became corrupt. Moses reminded God to remember the covenant they had made. We, too, are in covenant with God. "The Lord changed his mind of the evil he thought to do until his people, or the disaster had threatened" (Exodus 32:13 NLT).

Put God in remembrance of his Word. The blood is bagging up the promises. You can be healed through the covenant. The covenant can get you out of trouble, out of debt. Let us plead and reason together that you may be justified. The covenant can save your marriage. "Now if you obey me my treasured possession, although the whole earth is mine" (Exodus 19:5 KJV). Hebrews 8:6: "But in fact the ministry Jesus has received is as superior to theirs as the covenant of which he is mediator is superior to the old one, since the new covenant is established on better promises" (NIV).

CHAPTER 14

It's Finished

I thank you, God, for walking and talking to me as I wrote all these chapters and went through the process of completing Your plan. You were there during the good and the bad, on the rainy and sunshiny days. I was cursing and disobedient at first as I began Your special and unique assignment. Hallelujah, Daddy God! It's done! I have finished.

To You, God, be all the glory. You gave us the victory. Yes, we can win, but we have to keep steady till it's finished, no matter how many distractions we face. We have to look disappointment in the face and say, "I will live through it!"

I thank God I'm able to love Susan and forgive her for all the pain and hurt that we have gone through. Susan and I get along very well now. We sometimes talk on the phone when we need to. We talk maturely and respectfully to each other. We attend the grandchildren's birthday parties, and we have a lot of laughs together. We celebrate the children with love and support. My husband is amazed! He says, "Wow—peace after all!" He still finds it hard to believe that I refused to quit. I said, "It's because of God. I can't die and meet God face to face with the mission that He gave me unfinished. And He talked to me all the way through it."

I meet people as I go through my daily life. I hear comments like these: "You all did a wonderful job raising your sons, girl. Hats off!" "I applaud you for sticking in there. I remember all you went through with Susan."

"How is Susan? How is Abraham doing?" "Do you ever see Susan?" When I say, "Yes, she is doing great. She's not the same," I hear comments like this: "Girl, I bet she thanks God for you all now!" I say, "Yes, she does. She is appreciative now that we stepped in and took care of our sons."

New Direction: The Connection

400 Chocolate Lane Avenue, Huntsville, Alabama

We're still at our church, New Direction the Connection, with our great Dr. D. Jackson as our senior leader, and his wife, Dr. Chermaine Jackson. Abraham and I work in ministry. We enjoy life serving the people of God. We teach classes, sing on the praise team, serve on the prayer team, work with the children's church ministry and the men's ministry. We love our church family. The Word goes forward with power and conviction. It is sharper than a two-edge sword, and then it heals and delivers us and causes us to be transformed, having a renewed mind. Therefore, we can live victorious in this wonderful country God has given us to live in. Our lives have changed. My Bible still doesn't seem like the same one I had during my beginning years.

I thank God for Dr. D. Jackson, our senior pastor, the man God used to help change our family lives through the preaching of the gospel. Some of his most memorable life-changing sermons include "We Will Not Live Defeated," "Faith Works When You Work It," and "Kingdom Living." I do thank God for putting Dr. D. Jackson in our lives to teach us the Word, just as we needed. We have learned not to live a defeated life.

Special thanks to my loving sister Shaneese. I dreamed of my husband first, and later on she told me about a guy she had skated with. He told her he wanted to meet me. He was the guy in the dream. Sister, thanks for all your encouragement.

A special thanks to my big brother, Pastor Maurice Reynolds of Mt. Love More Baptist Church in Monroe, New Jersey, who officiated at our wedding on July 15, 1990. Brother, you encouraged me to persevere and stay on my mission. You said to me, "Sarah, it will soon be over. Ten to twelve years will go by fast. God told you to do this. He showed you your husband before you met him. Sis, this has been ordered by God. You can't quit this no matter how hard it is. God is your strength. You stay in the Word. You'll make it!" Thanks, big brother. I love you!

I'm also thankful for an incredible lady who has encouraged me since I met her. Dr. Renae Johnson is a friend and mentor who allowed me to use her as a guinea pig when I was in beauty school. She supported my salon business until I moved to Memphis. My long-time friend for over 30 years.

I extend a special thanks to Prophetess Marres. I met Adel and her family many years ago. Thank you for tutoring our sons three times a week and encouraging a love for learning. Thanks also for the dinners you served our sons along with your family. Adel would not allow me to pay her. In return, I asked if I could do her hair and her daughters' hair, and she said yes. Thanks for being a blessing to us. (I say this in loving memory.)

I'd also like to thank all those who prayed for me and all those who supported my salon during those years. You all made me laugh some seasons, and some seasons you made me cry, but it was all for my making. Romans 8:28: "And we know that all things work together for good to them that love God, to them who are called according to his purpose" (KJV).

Special thanks to Mrs. Lilly Tate for the encouraging words you gave, and your love and your support many times. Thank you for the days we cried together. Thank you, woman of God! Love you.

Special thanks to Mrs. Carrie Satchel. This lovely lady would call me days before she came to the salon for her hair service and say, "Sarah, don't cook for the boys. I'm cooking my special spaghetti with polish sausage and garlic bread." We were so glad to get it. I didn't have to put any food in the Crock-Pots on those days! It was a blessing and very kind of you to do that for us so many times. Thank you, woman of God!

Special thanks to Mrs. Aden Filer for typing my manuscript. I am so appreciative for your time. May God continue to shine on you. Many blessing to you!

For legal reasons, I could not mention the real names of our friends and family in this book; neither could we include their pictures. We love all of you! May God continue to "make his face shine on you and be gracious to you" (Numbers 6:25 NIV).

Grand Finale

Father, thank you for entrusting me, this unqualified servant girl, to do such a magnificent and incredible mission. I was only an instrument being used. Only You could have made this happen and given me the victory through it all. I'm smiling now. I pray I can continue to make You smile. As I make this new journey with this book, thank you, Lord!

Recommendation Letters

I was a witness to this story. I saw Sarah as she started her morning, stopping in with the children at the Circle K several times a week on her way taking them to school. I knew she was a business owner, and I wondered how she was doing so much. What she did was remarkable. I saw the end result. All I can say is, "Well done, sister." The world said it could not be done, but she has proven it can be done. With God, all things are possible. I recommend this book to all.

—Mr. Thomas Monroe

I've known Sarah all her life. She grew up in the church I attended. I was her children's choir director. I watched her grow and become a nice young lady. I remember when she married Abraham. I also remember when, a few years later, they received custody of his four boys. I remember when she was going through the struggle with Abraham's ex. It was always a hill for them to climb, always some nonsense; nevertheless, I could see the love she had for them. It showed on her face. She did her best concerning her family. Christ lived in this young lady. She loved God, and she had a glow. They would bring the children to church every Sunday. The boys were dressed well, and they were always clean.

I can't wait to get this book, I know it will be truthful and from the heart. I think everyone who reads this book will find it to be a blessing.

God Bless Abraham and Sarah

—Jalia James

A Salvation Prayer

Lord, I admit that I have done things that are wrong. Thank You for dying to take away all my sins. Please forgive me. I receive Your forgiveness now and declare that I want to live for You for the rest of my life with your Holy Spirit. I now depend completely on You. Amen.

If you have prayed this prayer, tell somebody else as soon as possible. (Don't wait.) Part of coming to faith in God is sharing your experience with others.

Asking God to save you is part of the journey of faith. There is much to learn! Jesus wants you to be his disciples, which means that we must follow him and learn from him:

- Be open to hear God speak into your life every day.
- Find out more about the life and teaching of Christ.
- Join with other Christians in worshipping and serving God.

Theme song: "Fathers, Rise Up"

ABOUT THE AUTHOR

Sarah Haley is a black African-American female native from Decatur, Al. She is the eighth child of ten siblings. She is the wife of Abraham Haley, for thirty amazing years. They raised four wonderful sons by faith, being led by the Holy Spirit. She was not the biological mother, had many highs and lows but she got the victory in the end.

Sarah was the first lady to preach in the pulpit at the church that she attended in 1996. She prayed and stood in faith for the Senior Pastor, who did not believe in women preachers it was a miracle…. the door open up for many more ladies afterwards. She know God hears her prayers and she get results!!

Sarah is a lead vocalist and sings on the praise and worship team at her church, and has recorded 3 songs in the studio in Memphis, Tn. She also works in children church ministry. She loves music and singing. She is fired up for Jesus!!

Sarah opened a Salon called Sarah's Magic Shears in 1990 at age 25. She has been a hair stylist for 33 years and has a Master Degree in Biblical Studies from Wilmington North Carolina College of Theology in 2009.

Sarah will find a way to share the word of God with much enthusiasm with everyone she meets throughout the day. She has been a witness for many years and loves it!

You can contact her at:
sarahhaley826@yahoo.com

Printed in the United States
By Bookmasters